The Little Book of Bathroom Meditations

THE LITTLE BOOK OF

Bathroom Meditations

spiritual wisdom for every day

MICHELLE HELLER

FAIR WINDS
PRESS
GLOUCESTER, MASSACHUSETTS

Text © 2003 Michelle Heller

First published in the USA in 2003 by
Fair Winds Press
33 Commercial Street
Gloucester, MA 01930

Library of Congress Cataloging-in-Publication Data available

ISBN 1-59233-028-2

10 9 8 7 6 5 4 3 2 1

Cover design by: Peter King & Company
Book design by: Peter King & Company

Printed and bound in Canada

Dedication

To the memory of my grandfather, H. Lee Baker,
whose nobility, kindness, wit, and spiritual
curiosity inspired all who knew him.

Acknowledgments

I would like to thank Phil Tavares and
Wendy Simard for their faith and encouragement.
Special gratitude goes to Brian Provenzale for
his tireless research efforts and, of course,
his ceaseless stream of tasteless potty humor.

contents

Part Three: The Mind

introduction

THE GODDESS OF THE LOO AND OTHER TIPS
FOR PASSING TIME IN THE LAVORATORY

The bathroom: where all men, great or small, must sooner or later face their own animal natures. But what exactly does the bathroom mean to us? The stark simplicity of a toilet bowl evokes a certain purity of purpose, and when sitting on the latrine, the human animal's intent is laid bare in a way that is downright endearing in this hurried, complicated world. The purpose of this book is to embrace that purity, to welcome the simple joy of relaxing on a seat of cool porcelain, unhurried and free from the worries of the world.

In the bathroom, all should take their time, but I firmly believe that it is not time that should go wasted. Bathroom time is precious—an invaluable section of space, however brief, which is ideal for asking ourselves that age-old question: Are we animal, or are we something more divine, more immortal? The next time you find yourself jarred by an unexpected sound or an unflattering odor, ask yourself: Does God want this? Would God create me as I am if He didn't? The collection of meditations, quotations, and philosophical ponderings that follow are intended to help you reflect on just that question, and any other deep contemplative matter you feel inclined to address. For many people, a bathroom session is their only chance for peace and privacy, so settle in and relax! It is one of the few occasions in a person's life when he is left alone, naked before God, as natural as the day he was born. So what better place to meditate on one's self and one's soul?

Cloacina

The Romans knew the importance of bathrooms—they even had a goddess, Cloacina, who was the patron of the city's public latrines and sewage systems. Not surprisingly, Cloacina was also the goddess of purification, and shrines were built around Rome to honor her and her processes of cleansing and expelling evil. The word "catharsis" comes to mind, with its dual meanings of emotional purification as well as purgation of bodily excrements. These twin meanings reflect the singular power of the bathroom activity to unite bodily functions with emotions: Indeed, bathrooms, toilets, and bowels each have a very strong emotional resonance for all of us.

As Cloacina can testify, bathroom time is not just about the body; the mind, the heart, and the spiritual self also have a role in every bathroom break. Why else do we still, even in the modern world, "bow down to the porcelain god"? Why else do we so relish this chance to purify ourselves? Perhaps it's because in the midst of this supremely natural act, where no one but ourselves and our god can see us, we are forced to face our natural selves as well as our spiritual selves. In the bathroom, the natural becomes the divine; people are closest to their truest selves, and are therefore most inclined to search for the truth, that cosmic truth of the toilet. Everyone knows that transcendent sense of release that follows a trip to the bathroom—is this sensation not a spiritual as well as a physical release? In bathrooms, men become animals, children, and angels all at once; Indeed it is the bathroom where mankind is perhaps at its most spiritual. Cloacina certainly would have thought so.

"Today I Broke Up a Marriage."

So bathrooms are places where people are most themselves, and nothing is a better reflection of this than a public restroom. The next time you're in a public bathroom, take a moment to study the latrinalia, or the graffiti found on the walls. Here people share secrets, boast sexual conquests, ask and offer advice, vow eternal love, and more often than not, pose tough philosophical questions. "Today I broke up a marriage," was the desperate confession I read in a bathroom a few months ago. "He's hot but he's kind of stupid. What should I do?" queried another troubled bathroomgoer. And her community responded, with advice, spiritual adages, and confessions of their own.

This confessional process in the bathroom is by no means a new ritual; Archeologists have in fact found evidence of graffiti in the ruins of ancient Roman latrines, scrawlings that often express the same concerns and emotions we find on restroom walls today. Throughout history, public bathrooms have been used as confessionals, therapist offices, and the site of illegal dealings, love-making sessions, nose-pickings, intimate conversations, and intense moral debates. But why is it that people feel the need to share their innermost thoughts, both trivial and philosophical, while in the loo? Maybe, like Rodin's "The Thinker," there's something about that particular physical posture that lends itself to intense meditation. "I do most of my work sitting down; that's where I shine," wrote writer Robert Benchley, and there's some truth to his correlation between physical relaxation and intellectual stimulation. More likely, though, bathroom-goers find themselves waxing philosophical simply because of the unbreakable link between bodily release and spiritual catharsis. In the bathroom, we are all equals and there is no room for judgment. The toilet as both confessional and psychiatrist's couch can in this way play an indispensable role in that purification process symbolized by old Cloacina.

The Neck of a Goose

Rich or poor, powerful or powerless, when we sit on a toilet we all look the same. The image of this strange juxtaposition—of how someone is in the outside world and how he is inside a bathroom—is why bathrooms are so inherently hilarious. But bathroom humor is not a new phenomenon: It has a long and esteemed literary history, from Chaucer through Swift on up to Bukowski. Medieval monk Francois Rabelais earned his bread—as well as his lifelong notoriety—through his bawdy tales of booze and bathrooms. In "Gargantua and Pantagruel," Gargantua explains in graphic detail his long search for the perfect toilet tissue. His hilarious tale recounts adventures with coverlets, curtains, satin handkerchiefs, spinach leaves, pillows, velvet hats, and even his mother's gloves, until he finally settles on the downy neck of a goose with which to wipe his bum. Writer Henry Miller also felt the need to celebrate the joys of the physical. In his twelve-page treatise in "Black Spring," he trumpets his love of peeing. "When I touch the subject of toilets I relive some of my best moments," he says, and then goes on to lovingly describe a few of the favorite urinals he's known in his lifetime. The comic aspects of the gutter is made clear in both these examples: Potty humor is a delicious and necessary affirmation of the animal known as man. So the next time you're on the john, laugh a little! There are few things funnier in life than a toilet bowl.

The quotations and passages in this book are intended to help you take advantage of your bathroom time. Organized into three parts—The Heart, The Body, and The Mind, it includes thoughts about the soul, nature, food and drink, humility, meditation, prayer, and laughter—all subjects that relate in one way or another to the precious, indestructible bond between mankind and his toilet. As William Shakespeare said, great floods have flown from simple sources, and so it is true in the bathroom. Great thoughts can indeed flow from simple bathroom sessions.

PART ONE:

the Heart

* * *

The bathroom is a great place to get in some hard thinking, but it's also a good spot in which to get in touch with your heart, your soul, and your spiritual self. The following selection of poetry, philosophical excerpts, adages, and biblical passages come from sources as diverse as da Vinci, Gandhi, philosopher William James, Mohammad Ali, the Dalai Lama, Elizabeth Barrett Browning, musician Leonard Cohen, Teresa of Avila, and actor Alan Alda. These writers, thinkers, and entertainers offer their thoughts on topics such as prayer, memory, awareness, marriage, courage, paganism, the elements of happiness, the necessity of laughter, and how to most appropriately give advice to a friend.

1. wisdom and prayer

The thousand mysteries around us would not trouble but interest us, if only we had cheerful, healthy hearts.

> — *Friedrich Nietzsche, 19th-century German philosopher*

The noblest pleasure is the joy of understanding.

> — *Leonardo da Vinci, 15th-century painter, sculptor, and inventor*

I do not feel obliged to believe that the same God who has endowed us with sense, reason, and intellect has intended us to forgo their use.

> — *Galileo Galilei, 17th-century Italian astronomer*

You must understand the whole of life, not just one little part of it. That is why you must read, that is why you must look at the skies, that is why you must sing and dance, and write poems and suffer and understand, for all that is life.

> — *Jiddu Krishnamurti, 20th-century Indian philosopher*

Honesty is the first chapter in the Book of Wisdom. Let it be our endeavor to merit the character of a just nation.

— Thomas Jefferson, American author and statesman

Sit down before fact as a little child, be prepared to give up every preconceived notion, follow humbly wherever and to whatever abysses nature leads, or you shall learn nothing.

— Thomas Henry Huxley, 19th-century English biologist

Be patient toward all that is unsolved in your heart and try to love the questions themselves. Live the questions now. Perhaps you will find them gradually, without noticing it, and live along some distant day into the answer.

— Rainer Maria Rilke, German poet and essayist

The stream of thought flows on; but most of its segments fall into the bottomless abyss of oblivion. Of some, no memory survives the instant of their passage. Of others, it is confined to a few moments, hours or days. Others, again, leave vestiges which are indestructible, and by means of which they may be recalled as long as life endures.

— William James, 19th-century American philosopher

Begin challenging your own assumptions. Your assumptions are your windows on the world. Scrub them off every once in a while, or the light won't come in.

— Alan Alda, American actor and director

The universe is change; our life is what our thoughts make it.

— Marcus Aurelius, 1st-century Roman emperor

There is much pleasure to be gained from useless knowledge.

— Bertrand Russell, British philosopher

Every man ought to be inquisitive through every hour of his great adventure down to the day when he shall no longer cast a shadow in the sun. For if he dies without a question in his heart, what excuse is there for his continuance?

— Frank Moore Colby, 18th-century American editor and essayist

Men are wise in proportion, not to their experience, but to their capacity for experience.

— James Boswell, 18th-century English biographer

A great many people think they are thinking when they are merely rearranging their prejudices.

> — *William James, 19th-century American philosopher*

Perhaps I am doomed to retrace my steps under the illusion that I am exploring, doomed to try and learn what I should simply recognize, learning a mere fraction of what I have forgotten.

> — *Andre Breton, French poet and critic*

Thoughts lead on to purposes; purposes go forth in action; actions form habits; habits decide character; and character fixes our destiny.

> — *Tryon Edwards, 19th-century American theologian and author*

Learning Zen is a phenomenon of gold and dung. Before you understand it, it's like gold; after you understand it, it's like dung.

> — *Zen master*

All great deeds and all great thoughts have a ridiculous beginning. Great works are often born on a street corner or in a restaurant's revolving door.

> — *Albert Camus, French novelist, playwright, and essayist*

The aim of life is to live, and to live means to be aware, joyously, drunkenly, serenely, divinely aware.

— Henry Miller, American author and essayist

In the midst of movement and chaos, keep stillness inside of you.

— Deepak Chopra, Indian author and physician

The plainest sign of wisdom is a continual cheerfulness: Her state is like that of things in the regions above the moon, always clear and serene.

— Michel de Montaigne, 16th-century French essayist

A man is what he thinks about all day long.

— Ralph Waldo Emerson, 19th-century American author and activist

Reflect on your present blessings, of which every man has many.

— Charles Dickens, English novelist

Meditation is to find out if there is a field which is not already contaminated by the known.

— Jiddu Krishnamurti, 20th-century Indian philosopher

One's first step in wisdom is to question everything and one's last is to come to terms with everything.

— *Georg Christoph Lichtenberg, 18th-century German educator, scientist, and writer*

Man's most human characteristic is not his ability to learn, which he shares with many other species, but his ability to teach and store what others have developed and taught him.

— *Margaret Meade, American anthropologist*

The wisdom of life consists in the elimination of nonessentials.

— *Lin Yutang, Chinese writer and philologist*

Resolve to be thyself; and know that who finds himself, loses his misery.

— *Matthew Arnold, 19th-century English poet*

The man who has no inner life is the slave of his surroundings.

— *Henri Frederic Amiel, 19th-century Swiss philosopher*

Nothing in life is to be feared. It is only to be understood.

— *Marie Curie, Polish physicist*

To be able to be caught up into the world of thought—that is to be educated.

— *Edith Hamilton, German-born author and classicist*

Learning without wisdom is a load of books on a donkey's back.

— *Zora Neale Hurston, American novelist*

The mind I love must still have wild places, a tangled orchard where dark damsons drop in the heavy grass, an overgrown little wood, the chance of a snake or two (real snakes), a pool that nobody's fathomed the depth of, and paths threaded with those little flowers planted by the mind.

— *Katherine Mansfield, New Zealand-born short-story writer*

By three methods we may learn wisdom: First, by reflection, which is noblest; second, by imitation, which is easiest; and third by experience, which is the bitterest.

— *Confucius, ancient Chinese philosopher*

Nothing contributes so much to tranquilize the mind as a steady purpose—a point on which the soul may fix its intellectual eye.

— *Mary Shelley, 19th-century English novelist*

To pray is to pay attention to something or someone other than oneself. Whenever a man so concentrates his attention—on a landscape, a poem, a geometrical problem, an idol, or the True God—that he completely forgets his own ego and desires, he is praying... The primary task of the schoolteacher is to teach children, in a secular context, the technique of prayer.

— *W.H. Auden, English poet*

Prayer is translation. A man translates himself into a child asking for all there is in a language he has barely mastered.

— *Leonard Cohen, Canadian singer/songwriter*

Prayer is not an old woman's idle amusement. Properly understood and applied, it is the most potent instrument of action.

— *Mohandas Gandhi, Indian statesman*

We may pray most when we say least, and we may pray least when we say most.

— *St. Augustine of Hippo, 4th-century Church Father*

Pray inwardly, even if you do not enjoy it. It does good, though you feel nothing. Yes, even though you think you are doing nothing.

    — *Julian of Norwich, 14th-century English anchoress, mystic, and author*

Prayer covers the whole of a man's life. There is no thought, feeling, yearning or desire, however low, trifling, or vulgar we may deem it, which, if it affects our real interest or happiness, we may not lay before God and be sure of sympathy. His nature is such that our often coming does not tire him. The whole burden of the whole life of every man may be rolled on to God and not weary him, though it has wearied the man.

    — *Henry Ward Beecher, 19th-century Protestant preacher and reformer*

Don't pray to escape trouble. Don't pray to be comfortable in your emotions. Pray to do the will of God in every situation. Nothing else is worth praying for.

    — *Samuel M. Shoemaker, American Episcopal rector*
    and cofounder of Alcoholics Anonymous

I have benefited by my praying for others; for by making an errand to God for them, I have gotten something for myself.

    — *Samuel Rutherford, 17th-century Scottish theologian and preacher*

In prayer, it is better to have heart without words, than words without heart. Prayer will make a man cease from sin, or sin entice a man to cease from prayer. The spirit of prayer is more precious than treasures of gold and silver. Pray often, for prayer is a shield to the soul, a sacrifice to God, and a scourge for Satan.

— *John Bunyan, 17th-century religious writer*

Prayer is not overcoming God's reluctance, but laying hold of His willingness.

— *Martin Luther, Protestant reformer*

Prayer should be the key of the day and the lock of the night.

— *Charles Haddon Spurgeon, 19th-century Baptist preacher*

Have you any days of fasting and prayer? Storm the throne of grace and persevere therein, and mercy will come down.

— *John Wesley, 17th-century reformer and founder of Methodism*

Perhaps you will have to spend hours on your knees or upon your face before the throne. Never mind. Wait. God will do great things for you if you will wait for Him. Yield to Him. Cooperate with Him.

— *John Smyth, 16th-century English Protestant reformer*

The story is told of a little guy valiantly but futilely trying to move a heavy log to clear a pathway to his favorite hideout. His dad stood nearby and finally asked him why he wasn't using all his strength. The little guy assured his dad he was straining with all his might. His dad quietly told him he was not using all his strength, because he hadn't asked him (his dad) to help.

— *Zig Zigler, American motivational speaker and author*

But when you pray, go into your room, close the door and pray to your Father, who is unseen. Then your Father, who sees what is done in secret, will reward you.

— *Matthew 6:6*

Prayer is not a substitute for work, thinking, watching, suffering, or giving; prayer is a support for all other efforts.

— *George Buttrick, English-born Presbyterian pastor, educator, and writer*

Our praying, however, needs to be pressed and pursued with an energy that never tires, a persistency which will not be denied, and a courage which never fails.

— *E.M. Bounds, 19th-century American Methodist minister*

God does nothing but by prayer, and everything with it.

— John Wesley, 17th-century reformer and founder of Methodism

Prayer does not fit us for the greater work; prayer is the greater work.

— Oswald Chambers, 19th-century Scottish minister, teacher, and author

More things are wrought by prayer than this world dreams of.

— Alfred, Lord Tennyson, English poet

2. love and friendship

To love another person is to see the face of God.

— *Victor Hugo, 19th-century French poet and novelist*

Love sought is good, but given unsought is better.

— *William Shakespeare, English playwright and poet*

For one human being to love another; that is perhaps the most difficult of our tasks, the ultimate, the last test and proof, the work for which all other work is but preparation.

— *Rainer Maria Rilke, German poet and essayist*

A very small degree of hope is sufficient to cause the birth of love.

— *Stendhal, 19th-century French novelist*

Love is a canvas furnished by Nature and embroidered by imagination.

— *Voltaire, French Enlightenment writer*

The best portion of a good man's life is his little, nameless unremembered acts of kindness and of love.

— *William Wordsworth, English Romantic poet*

I don't want to live—I want to love first and live incidentally.

— *Zelda Fitzgerald, American writer and wife of F. Scott Fitzgerald*

If I speak in the tongues of men and of angels, but have not love, I am only a resounding gong or a clanging cymbal. If I have the gift of prophecy and can fathom all mysteries and all knowledge, and if I have a faith that can move mountains, but have not love, I am nothing. If I give all I possess to the poor and surrender my body to the flames, but have not love I gain nothing. Love is patient, love is kind. It does not envy, it does not boast, it is not proud. It is not rude, it is not self-seeking, it is not easily angered, it keeps no record of wrongs. Love does not delight in evil but rejoices with the truth. It always protects, always trusts, always perseveres. Love never fails. But where there are prophecies, they will cease; where there are tongues, they will be stilled; where there is knowledge, it will pass away... and now these things remain: faith, hope and love. But the greatest of these is love.

— *Corinthians 13:1-8, 13*

Love is life. And if you miss love, you miss life.

— *Leo Buscaglia, American author, educator, and speaker*

Whenever you are confronted with an opponent, conquer him with love.

— *Mohandas Gandhi, Indian statesman*

Marriage and deathless friendship, both should be inviolable and sacred: two great creative passions, separate, apart, but complementary: the one pivotal, the other adventurous: the one, marriage, the centre of human life; and the other, the leap ahead.

— *D.H. Lawrence, English novelist and poet*

The greatest love is a mother's; then comes a dog's; then comes a sweetheart's.

— *Polish proverb*

Love (understood as the desire of good for another) is in fact so unnatural a phenomenon that it can scarcely repeat itself, the soul being unable to become virgin again and not having energy enough to cast itself out again into the ocean of another's soul.

— *James Joyce, Irish novelist*

True friendship's laws are by this rule express'd,
Welcome the coming, speed the parting guest.

— Alexander Pope, 18th-century English poet

All thoughts, all passions, all delights
Whatever stirs this mortal frame
All are but ministers of Love
And feed his sacred flame.

— Samuel Taylor Coleridge, English poet

If I place love above everything, it is because for me it is the most
desperate, the most despairing state of affairs imaginable.

— Andre Breton, French poet and critic

I have found the paradox that if I love until it hurts, then there is no
hurt, but only more love.

— Mother Teresa, Roman Catholic nun and missionary

Love is the most difficult and dangerous form of courage. Courage is
the most desperate, admirable and noble kind of love.

— Delmore Schwartz, American poet and writer

By all means marry. If you get a good wife you will become happy, and if you get a bad one you will become a philosopher.

— Socrates, ancient Greek philosopher

They say love is blind... and marriage is an institution. Well, I'm not ready for an institution for the blind just yet.

— Mae West, American film actress

Was she so loved because her eyes were so beautiful, or were her eyes so beautiful because she was so loved?

— Anzia Yenerska, Polish writer

Everything is clearer when you're in love.

— John Lennon, English singer/songwriter

Let your love be like the misty rain, coming softly, but flooding the river.

— Madagascan proverb

Self-love, my liege, is not so vile a sin as self-neglecting.

— William Shakespeare, English playwright and poet

He that shuts love out, in turn shall be shut out from love, and on her threshold lie, howling in outer darkness.

— *Alfred, Lord Tennyson, English poet*

Life is the flower of which love is the honey.

— *Victor Hugo, 19th-century French poet and novelist*

Love has nothing to do with what you are expecting to get—only what you are expecting to give—which is everything. What you will receive in return varies. But it really has no connection with what you give. You give because you love and cannot help giving.

— *Katharine Hepburn, American actress*

There's nothing in this world so sweet as love, and next to love the sweetest thing is hate.

— *Henry Wadsworth Longfellow, 19th-century American poet*

True friendship multiplies the good in life and divides its evils. Strive to have friends, for life without friends is like life on a desert island... to find one real friend in a lifetime is good fortune; to keep him is a blessing.

— *Baltasar Gracian, 17th-century Spanish philosopher*

The usual (and very vicious) nonsense preached on the subject of love claims that love is self-sacrifice. A man's self is his spirit. If one sacrifices his spirit, who or what is left to feel the love? True love is profoundly selfish, in the noblest meaning of the word—it is an expression of one's self, of one's highest values. When a person is in love, he seeks his own happiness—and not his sacrifice to the loved one. And the loved one would be a monster if she wanted or expected sacrifice.

— *Ayn Rand, Russian-born novelist and philosopher*

No soul is desolate as long as there is a human being for whom it can feel trust and reverence.

— *George Eliot, 19th-century English novelist*

Two are better than one; because they have a good reward for their labour. For if they fall, the one will lift up his fellow: but woe to him that is alone when he falleth; for he hath not another to help him up.

— *Ecclesiastes 4:9*

When friends stop being frank and useful to each other, the whole world loses some of its radiance.

— *Anatole Broyard, American literary critic and essayist*

Nearly all marriages, even happy ones, are mistakes: in the sense that almost certainly (in a more perfect world, or even with a little more care in this very imperfect one) both partners might be found more suitable mates. But the real soulmate is the one you are actually married to.

— *J.R.R. Tolkien, British writer and scholar*

The greatest happiness in life is the conviction that we are loved—loved for ourselves, or rather, loved in spite of ourselves.

— *Victor Hugo, 19th-century French poet and novelist*

Friendship is always a sweet responsibility; never an opportunity.

— *Kahlil Gibran, Lebanese-born poet and novelist*

There is an important difference between love and friendship. While the former delights in extremes and opposites, the latter demands equality.

— *Françoise d'Aubigné Maintenon, wife of Louis XIV of France*

There is no hope of joy except in human relations.

— *Antoine de Sainte-Exupery, French writer*

In giving advice, seek to help, not to please, your friend.

— Solon, Athenian statesman and poet

Friendship is one of the sweetest joys of life. Many might have failed beneath the bitterness of their trial had they not found a friend.

— Charles Haddon Spurgeon, 19th-century Baptist preacher

Friendship is unnecessary, like philosophy, like art. It has no survival value; rather it is one of those things that give value to survival.

— C.S. Lewis, English novelist and critic

And when love speaks, the voice of all the gods makes heaven drowsy with the harmony.

— William Shakespeare, English playwright and poet

Friendship is the hardest thing in the world to explain. It's not something you learn in school. But if you haven't learned the meaning of friendship, you really haven't learned anything.

— Muhammad Ali, American boxer

Friendship that flows from the heart cannot be frozen by adversity, as the water that flows from the spring cannot congeal in winter.

— *James Fenimore Cooper, 19th-century American novelist*

Don't flatter yourself that friendship authorizes you to say disagreeable things to your intimates. The nearer you come into relation with a person, the more necessary do tact and courtesy become.

— *Oliver Wendell Holmes, American lawyer and judge*

Thus nature has no love for solitude, and always leans, as it were, on some support; and the sweetest support is found in the most intimate friendships.

— *Marcus Cicero, Roman orator and writer*

The world is like a mirror, you see? Smile, and your friends smile back.

— *Zen proverb*

To infinite, ever present Love, all is Love, and there is no error, no sin sickness, nor death.

— *Mary Baker Eddy, writer and founder of Christian Science*

It's the friends you can call up at 4 A.M. that matter.

— Marlene Dietrich, German actress

We are all travelers in the wilderness of this world, and the best that we can find in our travels is an honest friend.

— Robert Louis Stevenson, 19th-century Scottish author

True friendship is like sound health; the value of it is seldom known until it be lost.

— Charles Caleb Colton, 19th-century English clergyman and writer

An honest answer is the sign of true friendship.

— Proverbs 24:26

My best friend is the one who brings out the best in me.

— Henry Ford, inventor and industrialist

It is a sweet thing, friendship, a dear balm,
A happy and auspicious bird of calm.

— Percy Bysshe Shelley, English poet

My friends are my estate.

— Emily Dickinson, American poet

The better part of one's life consists of his friendships.

— Abraham Lincoln, American president and lawyer

Two may talk together under the same roof for many years, yet never really meet; and two others at first speech are old friends.

— Mary Catherwood, 19th-century American author

Make new friends and keep the old, one is silver and the other gold.

— Girl Scout saying

The greatest good you can do for another is not just share your riches, but to reveal to him, his own.

— Benjamin Disraeli, 19th-century novelist and British prime minister

Treat people as if they were what they ought to be and you help them to become what they are capable of being.

— Johann Wolfgang von Goethe, German poet and novelist

Anybody can sympathize with the sufferings of a friend, but it requires a very fine nature to sympathize with a friend's success.

— *Oscar Wilde, 19th-century Irish poet and playwright*

Friendship with oneself is all-important because without it one cannot be friends with anyone else in the world.

— *Eleanor Roosevelt, American activist and First Lady*

The friendship that can cease has never been real.

— *St. Jerome, 4th-century Christian ascetic*

I find friendship to be like wine, raw when new, ripened with age, the true old man's milk and restorative cordial.

— *Thomas Jefferson, American author and statesman*

Without friends no one would choose to live, though he had all other goods.

— *Aristotle, ancient Greek philosopher*

A real friend is one who walks in when the rest of the world walks out.

— *Walter Winchell, newspaper columnist*

I no doubt deserved my enemies, but I don't believe I deserved my friends.

— *Walt Whitman, American poet*

Dignity and love do not blend well, nor do they continue long together.

— *Ovid, ancient Roman poet*

Love is eternal—the aspect may change, but not the essence. There is the same difference in a person before and after he is in love as there is in an unlighted lamp and one that is burning. The lamp was there and was a good lamp, but now it is shedding light too, and that is its real function. And love makes one calmer about many things, and that way, one is more fit for one's work.

— *Vincent van Gogh, Dutch painter*

3. laughter and happiness

At the height of laughter, the universe is flung into a kaleidoscope of new possibilities.

— Jean Houston, American psychologist and mythologist

Laughter is the most healthful exertion.

— Christoph Wilhelm Hufeland, 18th-century German physician and writer

'Tis a good thing to laugh at any rate; and if a straw can tickle a man, it is an instrument of happiness.

— John Dryden, 17th-century English poet

The most wasted of all days is one without laughter.

— e.e. cummings, American poet

Laughter is one of the very privileges of reason, being confined to the human species.

— Thomas Carlyle, 19th-century Scottish scholar and writer

If taking vitamins doesn't keep you healthy enough, try more laughter:
The most wasted of all days is that on which one has not laughed.

— *Nicolas-Sebastien Chamfort, 18th-century French writer and humorist*

God is a comedian playing to an audience too afraid to laugh.

— *Voltaire, French Enlightenment writer*

Total absence of humor renders life impossible.

— *Colette, French novelist*

Laugh at yourself first, before anyone else can.

— *Elsa Maxwell, actress, socialite, and humorist*

Laughter gives us distance. It allows us to step back from an event, deal with it and then move on.

— *Bob Newhart, American comedian*

Always laugh when you can. It is cheap medicine.

— *Lord Byron, English Romantic poet*

You can't deny laughter; when it comes, it plops down in your favorite chair and stays as long as it wants.

— *Stephen King, American horror writer*

Beware of too much laughter, for it deadens the mind and produces oblivion.

— *The Talmud*

A person without a sense of humor is like a wagon without springs, jolted by every pebble in the road.

— *Henry Ward Beecher, 19th-century Protestant preacher and reformer*

Laughter is the shortest distance between two people.

— *Victor Borge, Danish actor and comedian*

Perhaps I know why it is man alone who laughs: He alone suffers so deeply that he had to invent laughter.

— *Friedrich Nietzsche, 19th-century German philosopher*

Man thinks. God laughs.

— *Jewish proverb*

No man who has once heartily and wholly laughed can be altogether irreclaimably bad.

— *Thomas Carlyle, 19th-century Scottish scholar and writer*

To listen to some devout people, one would imagine that God never laughs.

— *Ghose Aurobindo, Indian nationalist and philosopher*

When one door of happiness closes, another opens. But often we look so long at the closed door we do not see the one which has been opened to us.

— *Helen Keller, writer and activist for the disabled*

Happiness is having a large, loving, caring, close-knit family in another city.

— *George Burns, American comedian*

We are never so happy or so unhappy as we think.

— *François duc de La Rochefoucauld, 17th-century French writer and memoirist*

Now and then it's good to pause in our pursuit of happiness and just be happy.

— *Guillaume Apollinaire, Italian-born French poet and critic*

Acting happier than you feel can make you happier than you are.

— Fran Lebowitz, American humorist

The pursuit of happiness is a most ridiculous phrase; if you pursue happiness you'll never find it.

— Charles Percy Snow, English novelist and scientist

Happiness is a how, not a what; a talent, not an object.

— Hermann Hesse, German novelist

We must select the illusion which appeals to our temperament, and embrace it with passion, if we want to be happy.

— Cyril Connolly, 20th-century English writer

Happiness is a warm puppy.

— Charles Schulz, American cartoonist

Happiness makes up in height for what it lacks in length.

— Robert Frost, American poet

For most of life, nothing wonderful happens. If you don't enjoy getting up and working and finishing your work and sitting down to a meal with family or friends, then the chances are that you're not going to be very happy. If someone bases his happiness or unhappiness on major events like a great new job, huge amounts of money, a flawlessly happy marriage or a trip to Paris, that person isn't going to be happy much of the time. If, on the other hand, happiness depends on a good breakfast, flowers in the yard, a drink or a nap, then we are more likely to live with quite a bit of happiness.

— *Andy Rooney, American writer and humorist*

For every moment of triumph, for every instance of beauty, many souls must be trampled.

— *Hunter S. Thompson, American writer*

Happiness lies only in that which excites, and the only thing that excites is crime.

— *Marquis de Sade, 18th-century French writer*

We all live with the objective of being happy; our lives are all different and yet the same.

— *Anne Frank, German-born Jewish diarist*

Sooner or later in life everyone discovers that perfect happiness is unrealizable, but there are few who pause to consider the antithesis: that perfect unhappiness is equally unattainable.

— *Primo Levi, Italian Jewish writer and poet*

How are the waters of the world sweet—if we should die, we have drunk them. If we should sin—or separate—if we should fail or succeed —we have tasted of happiness—we must be written in the book of the blessed. We have had what life could give, we have eaten of the tree of knowledge, we have known—we have been the mystery of the universe.

— *John Jay Chapman, American poet and critic*

The secret of happiness is this: Let your interests be as wide as possible, and let your reactions to the things and persons that interest you be as far as possible friendly rather than hostile.

— *Bertrand Russell, British philosopher*

Once my heart was captured, reason was shown the door, deliberately and with a sort of frantic joy. I accepted everything, I believed everything, without struggle, without suffering, without regret, without false shame. How can one blush for what one adores?

— *George Sand, 19th-century French novelist*

Did you ever see an unhappy horse? Did you ever see a bird that has the blues? One reason why birds and horses are not unhappy is because they are not trying to impress other birds and horses.

— *Dale Carnegie, writer and motivational speaker*

It is the chiefest point of happiness that a man is willing to be what he is.

— *Desiderius Erasmus, Dutch writer and Humanist*

Nine requisites for contented living: Health enough to make work a pleasure. Wealth enough to support your needs. Strength to battle with difficulties and overcome them. Grace enough to confess your sins and forsake them. Patience enough to toil until some good is accomplished. Charity enough to see some good in your neighbor. Love enough to move you to be useful and helpful to others. Faith enough to make real the things of God. Hope enough to remove all anxious fears concerning the future.

— *Johann Wolfgang von Goethe, German poet and novelist*

Ancient Egyptians believed that upon death they would be asked two questions and their answers would determine whether they could continue their journey in the afterlife. The first question was, "Did you bring joy?" The second was, "Did you find joy?"

— *Leo Buscaglia, American author, educator, and speaker*

The best things in life are nearest: breath in your nostrils, light in your eyes, flowers at your feet, duties at your hand, the path of right just before you. Then do not grasp at the stars, but do life's plain, common work as it comes, certain that daily duties and daily bread are the sweetest things in life.

— *Robert Louis Stevenson, 19th-century Scottish author*

All the art of living lies in a fine mingling of letting go and holding on.

— *Havelock Ellis, English sexologist*

There are three ingredients to the good life: learning, earning, and yearning.

— *Christopher Morley, American novelist and essayist*

When you are sorrowful, look again in your heart, and you shall see that in truth you are weeping for that which has been your delight.

— *Kahlil Gibran, Lebanese-born poet and novelist*

Who is wise? He that learns from every One. Who is powerful? He that governs his Passions. Who is rich? He that is content. Who is that? Nobody.

— *Benjamin Franklin, American writer, scientist, and statesman*

Happiness is nothing more than good health and a bad memory.

— *Albert Schweitzer, German physician and theologian*

Look up, laugh loud, talk big, keep the color in your cheek and the fire in your eye, adorn your person, maintain your health, your beauty and your animal spirits.

— *William Hazlitt, 18th-century English essayist*

Coarse rice for food, water to drink, and the bended arm for a pillow— happiness may be enjoyed even in these.

— *Confucius, ancient Chinese philosopher*

If your daily life seems poor, do not blame it; blame yourself that you are not poet enough to call forth its riches; for the Creator, there is no poverty.

— *Rainer Maria Rilke, German poet and essayist*

Happiness is spiritual, born of Truth and Love. It is unselfish; therefore it cannot exist alone, but requires all mankind to share it.

— *Mary Baker Eddy, writer and founder of Christian Science*

Wisdom is the supreme part of happiness.

— Sophocles, ancient Greek playwright

The grand essentials to happiness in this life are something to do, something to love, and something to hope for.

— Joseph Addison, 17th-century English essayist

Knowing others is intelligence; knowing yourself is true wisdom. Mastering others is strength; mastering yourself is true power. If you realize that you have enough, you are truly rich.

— The Tao Te Ching

Himself is the source of the best and most a man can be or achieve. The more this is so—the more a man finds his sources of pleasure in himself—the happier he will be. For all other sources of happiness are in their nature most uncertain.

— Arthur Schopenhauer, Polish-born 19th-century philosopher

Happiness is a thing to be practiced, like the violin.

— John Lubbock, 19th-century English anthropologist, biologist, and essayist

It is the great privilege of poverty to be happy and yet unenvied, secure without a guard, and to obtain from the bounty of nature what the great and wealthy are compelled to procure by the help of art.

— *Samuel Johnson, 18th-century lexicographer and critic*

Whether one believes in religion or not, whether one believes in this religion or that religion, the very purpose of our life is happiness, the very motion of our life is towards happiness.

— *The Dalai Lama, 14th spiritual leader of Tibet*

Drink and dance and laugh and lie,
Love, the reeling midnight through,
for tomorrow we shall die!
(But, alas, we never do.)

— *Dorothy Parker, American poet and humorist*

4. the soul and visions of the infinite

If I have any beliefs about immortality, it is that certain dogs I have known will go to heaven, and very, very few persons.

— *James Thurber, American humorist*

For what is mysticism? Is it not the attempt to draw near to God, not by rites or ceremonies, but by inward disposition? Is it not merely a hard word for "The Kingdom of Heaven is within"?... Heaven is neither a place nor a time.

— *Florence Nightingale, Italian-born 19th-century nurse*

There is nothing new. All men know it at those rare moments when the soul sobers herself, and leaves off her chattering and protesting and insisting about this formula or that. In the silence of our theories we then seem to listen, and to hear something like the pulse of Being beat; and it is borne in upon us that the mere turning of the character, the dumb willingness to serve this universe, is more than all theories about it put together.

— *William James, 19th-century American philosopher*

Think, in mounting higher,
The angels would press on us, and aspire
To drop some golden orb of perfect song
Into our deep, dear silence.

— Elizabeth Barrett Browning, 19th-century English poet

The soul fortunately, has an interpreter—often an unconscious, but still a truthful interpreter—in the eye.

— Charlotte Bronte, 19th-century English novelist

Oh may I join the choir invisible
Of those immortal dead who live again
In minds made better by their presence.

— George Eliot, 19th-century English novelist

The soul should always stand ajar, ready to welcome the ecstatic experience.

— Emily Dickinson, American poet

I took a deep breath and listened to the old bray of my heart. I am. I am. I am.

— Sylvia Plath, American poet

The miracles of the church seem to me to rest not so much upon faces or voices or healing power coming suddenly near to us from afar off, but upon our perceptions being made finer, so that for a moment our eyes can see and our ears can hear what is there about us always.

— *Willa Cather, 19th-century American novelist*

This most beautiful system [the universe] could only proceed from the dominion of an intelligent and powerful Being.

— *Isaac Newton, 17th-century physicist*

Why not let people differ about their answers to the great mysteries of the Universe? Let each seek one's own way to the highest, to one's own sense of supreme loyalty in life, one's ideal of life. Let each philosophy, each worldview bring forth its truth and beauty to a larger perspective, that people may grow in vision, stature and dedication.

— *Algernon Black, English occult novelist*

There is no God.
But it does not matter.
Man is enough.

— *Edna St. Vincent Millay, American poet*

All things must come to the soul from its roots, from where it is planted. The tree that is beside the running water is fresher and gives more fruit.

— *Teresa of Avila, 16th-century Spanish saint and mystic*

It appears to me impossible that I should cease to exist, or that this active, restless spirit, equally alive to joy and sorrow, should be only organized dust—ready to fly abroad the moment the spring snaps, or the spark goes out, which kept it together. Surely something resides in this heart that is not perishable—and life is more than a dream.

— *Mary Wollstonecraft, 18th-century essayist and feminist*

Man alone knows that he must die; but that very knowledge raises him, in a sense, above mortality, by making him a sharer in the vision of eternal truth. He becomes the spectator of his own tragedy; he sympathizes so much with the fury of the storm that he has no ears left for the shipwrecked sailor, though the sailor were his own soul. The truth is cruel, but it can be loved, and it makes free those who have loved it.

— *George Santayana, Spanish-born American philosopher and critic*

Give beauty back, back to God, beauty's self and beauty's giver.

— *Gerard Manley Hopkins, 19th-century English religious poet*

Our birth is but a sleep and a forgetting:
The Soul that rises with us, our life's Star,
Hath had elsewhere its setting,
And cometh from afar.
Not in entire forgetfulness,
And not in utter nakedness,
But trailing clouds of glory do we come
From God, who is our home:
Heaven lies about us in our infancy!

— *William Wordsworth, English Romantic poet*

You are the music while the music lasts.

— *T.S. Eliot, American-born poet*

The majesty of God in itself goes beyond the capacity of human
understanding and cannot be comprehended by it... We must adore
its loftiness rather than investigate it, so that we do not remain
overwhelmed by so great a splendor.

— *John Calvin, 16th-century Protestant reformer*

One should be ever booted and spurred and ready to depart.

— *Michel de Montaigne, 16th-century French essayist*

They say that God is everywhere, and yet we always think of Him as somewhat of a recluse.

> — *Emily Dickinson, American poet*

We shall find peace. We shall hear angels. We shall see the sky sparkling with diamonds.

> — *Anton Chekhov, Russian playwright and short-story writer*

For life in the present there is no death. Death is not an event in life. It is not a fact in the world.

> — *Ludwig Wittgenstein, Austrian philosopher*

God will not suffer man to have a knowledge of things to come; for if he had prescience of his prosperity, he would be careless; and if understanding of his adversity, he would be despairing and senseless.

> — *St. Augustine of Hippo, 4th-century Church Father*

Human beings must be known to be loved; but Divine beings must be loved to be known.

> — *Blaise Pascal, 17th-century French mathematician and theologian*

This is my simple religion. There is no need for temples; no need for complicated philosophy. Our own brain, our own heart is our temple; the philosophy is kindness.

— The Dalai Lama, 14th spiritual leader of Tibet

One short sleep past will wake eternally
And death shall be no more;
Death thou shalt die.

— John Donne, 16th-century metaphysical poet

The angels play on their horns all day,
The whole earth in progression seems to pass by.
But does anyone hear the music they play,
Does anyone even try?

— Bob Dylan, American singer/songwriter

The gods, likening themselves to all kinds of strangers, go in various disguises from city to city, observing the wrongdoing and the righteousness of men.

— Homer, ancient Greek poet

Let every dawn be to you as the beginning of life, and every setting sun be to you as its close.

— *John Ruskin, 19th-century English writer and art critic*

The light you give off
Did not come from a pelvis
Your features did not begin in semen.
Don't try to hide inside anger
Radiance that cannot be hidden.

— *Rumi, 13th-century Persian poet*

Heaven must be an awfully dull place if the poor in spirit live there.

— *Emma Goldman, Lithuanian-born anarchist and activist*

In the attitude of silence the soul finds the path in a clearer light, and what is elusive and deceptive resolves itself into crystal clearness.

— *Mohandas Gandhi, Indian statesman*

My religion consists of a humble admiration of the illimitable superior spirit who reveals himself in the slight details we are able to perceive with our frail and feeble mind.

— *Albert Einstein, German-born American physicist*

To me heaven would be a big bull ring with me holding barrera seats and a trout stream outside that no one else was allowed to fish in and two lovely houses in the town; one where I would have my wife and children and be monogamous and love them truly and well and the other where I would have my nine beautiful mistresses on nine different floors and one would be fitted up with special copies of "The Dial" printed on soft tissue kept in the toilets on every floor and in the other house we would use "The American Mercury" and "The New Republic." Then there would be a fine church like in Pamplona where I could go and be confessed on the way from one house to the other and I would get on my horse and ride out with my son to the bull ranch named Hacienda Hadley and toss coins to all my illegitimate children that lived [along] the road. I would write out at the Hacienda and send my son in to lock the chastity belts onto my mistresses because someone had just galloped up with news that a notorious monogamist named Fitzgerald had been seen riding toward the town at the head of a company of strolling drinkers.

— *Ernest Hemingway, American novelist*

For I am convinced that neither death nor life, neither angels nor demons, neither the present not the future, nor any powers, neither height nor depth, nor anything else in all creation, will be able to separate us from the love of God.

— *Romans 8:38, 39*

Millions long for immortality who don't know what to do with themselves on a rainy Sunday afternoon.

— *Susan Ertz, American-born English novelist*

I am like a falling star who has finally found her place next to another in a lovely constellation, where we will sparkle in the heavens forever.

— *Amy Tan, American novelist*

Heaven is so far of the Mind
That were the Mind dissolved—
The Site—of it—by Architect
Could not again be proved—
'Tis vast—as our Capacity—
As fair—as our idea—
To Him of adequate desire
No further 'tis, than Here—

— *Emily Dickinson, American poet*

We do not believe in immortality because we can prove it, but we try to prove it because we cannot help believing it.

— *Harriet Martineau, 19th-century English novelist and journalist*

'Tis immortality to die aspiring,
As if a man were taken quick to heaven.

— George Chapman, 16th-century poet and playwright

One who sees the Supersoul accompanying the individual soul in all bodies and who understands that neither the soul nor the Supersoul is ever destroyed, actually sees.

— The Bhagavad Gita

The unique personality which is the real life in me, I can not gain unless I search for the real life, the spiritual quality, in others. I am myself spiritually dead unless I reach out to the fine quality dormant in others. For it is only with the god enthroned in the innermost shrine of the other, that the god hidden in me, will consent to appear.

— Felix Adler, 19th-century educator, social critic, and founder of The New York Society for Ethical Culture

Only barbarians are not curious about where they come from, how they came to be where they are, where they appear to be going, whether they wish to go there, and if so, why, and if not, why not.

— Isaiah Berlin, British philosopher

'Tis true; 'tis certain; man though dead retains
Part of himself; the immortal mind remains.

— Homer, ancient Greek poet

A soul is but the last bubble of a long fermentation in the world.

— George Santayana, Spanish-born American philosopher and critic

Beth could not reason upon or explain the faith that gave her courage and patience to give up life, and cheerfully wait for death. Like a confiding child, she asked no questions, but left everything to God and nature, Father and Mother of us all, feeling sure that they, and they only, could teach and strengthen heart and spirit for this life and the life to come.

— Louisa May Alcott, 19th-century American novelist

5. hope and faith

Hope is a thing with feathers
That perches in the soul,
And sings the tune without words
And never stops at all.

— *Emily Dickinson, American poet*

A dream is the bearer of a new possibility, the enlarged horizon, the great hope.

— *Howard Thurman, American educator and civil-rights leader*

The world is not yet exhausted; let me see something tomorrow which I never saw before.

— *Samuel Johnson, 18th-century lexicographer and critic*

I am not afraid of tomorrow, for I have seen yesterday and I love today.

— *William Allen White, American journalist and free-speech activist*

Hope in reality is the worst of all evils, because it prolongs the torments of man.

— Friedrich Nietzsche, 19th-century German philosopher

Yes, I have doubted. I have wandered off the path. I have been lost. But I always returned. It is beyond the logic I seek. It is intuitive—an intrinsic, built-in sense of direction. I seem always to find my way home. My faith has wavered but has saved me.

— Helen Hayes, American stage and screen actress

Without risk there is no faith. Faith is precisely the contradiction between the infinite passion of the individual's inwardness and the objective uncertainty.

— Soren Kierkegaard, 19th-century Danish philosopher and theologian

Doubt is part of all religion. All the religious thinkers were doubters.

— Isaac Bashevis Singer, Polish-born writer

Live out of your imagination instead of out of your memory.

— Les Brown, American bandleader and songwriter

Sometimes our fate resembles a fruit tree in winter. Who would think that those branches would turn green again and blossom, but we hope it, we know it.

— Johann Wolfgang von Goethe, German poet and novelist

No winter lasts forever; no spring skips its turn.

— Hal Borland, American columnist and nature writer

Now, God be praised, that to believing souls
Gives light in darkness, comfort in despair!

— William Shakespeare, English playwright and poet

All things are inconstant except the faith in the soul, which changes all things and fills their inconstancy with light, but though I seem to be driven out of my country as a misbeliever I have found no man yet with a faith like mine.

— James Joyce, Irish novelist

Sometimes I've believed as many as six impossible things before breakfast.

— Lewis Carroll, 19th-century English mathematician and children's writer

Consult not your fears but your hopes and your dreams. Think not about your frustrations, but about your unfulfilled potential. Concern yourself not with what you tried and failed in, but with what it is still possible for you to do.

— *Pope John XXIII*

Faith is like radar that sees through the fog—the reality of things at a distance that the human eye cannot see.

— *Corrie ten Boom, writer and member of the Dutch underground for Jewish refugees*

A garden is evidence of faith. It links us with all the misty figures of the past who also planted and were nourished by the fruits of their planting.

— *Gladys Taber, American novelist and short-story writer*

Every tomorrow has two handles. We can take hold of it with the handle of anxiety or the handle of faith.

— *Henry Ward Beecher, 19th-century Protestant preacher and reformer*

Take the first step in faith. You don't have to see the whole staircase, just take the first step.

— *Martin Luther King, Jr., Baptist minister and civil-rights leader*

Faithless is he that says farewell when the road darkens.

— J.R.R. Tolkien, British writer and scholar

Faith is the daring of the soul to go farther than it can see.

— William Newton Clarke, 19th-century American educator and religious philosopher

I am an idealist. I don't know where I'm going, but I'm on my way.

— Carl Sandburg, American poet

But groundless hope, like unconditional love, is the only kind worth having.

— John Perry Barlow, American lyricist and Internet activist

There are always flowers for those who want to see them.

— Henri Matisse, French painter

Turn your face to the sun and the shadows fall behind you.

— Maori proverb

There is surely a future hope for you, and your hope will not be cut off.

— Proverbs 23:18

A pessimist sees only the dark side of the clouds, and mopes; a philosopher sees both sides, and shrugs; an optimist doesn't see the clouds at all—he's walking on them.

— *Leonard Louis Levinson, American writer and humorist*

Idealism increases in direct proportion to one's distance from the problem.

— *John Galsworthy, English novelist*

An optimist is a man who has never had much experience.

— *Don Marquis, American humorist and newspaper columnist*

If you are here unfaithfully with us,
You're causing terrible damage.
If you've opened your loving to God's love,
You're helping people you don't know
And have never seen.

Is what I say true? Say yes quickly,
If you know, if you've known it
From before the beginning of the universe.

— *Rumi, 13th-century Persian poet*

As long as there is one upright man, as long as there is one compassionate woman, the contagion may spread and the scene is not desolate. Hope is the thing that is left to us, in a bad time. I shall get up Sunday morning and wind the clock, as a contribution to order and steadfastness.

— *E.B. White, American writer and editor*

Doubt is not a pleasant condition, but certainty is absurd.

— *Voltaire, French Enlightenment writer*

He who loses money, loses much; he who loses a friend, loses much more; he who loses faith, loses all.

— *Eleanor Roosevelt, American activist and First Lady*

Hope is itself a species of happiness, and, perhaps, the chief happiness which this world affords.

— *Samuel Johnson, 18th-century lexicographer and critic*

Above all, taking the shield of faith, wherewith ye shall be able to quench all the fiery darts of the wicked.

— *Ephesians 6:16*

Faith is not making religious-sounding noises in the daytime. It is asking your inmost self questions at night—and then getting up and going to work.

— *Mary Jean Irion, American writer and educator*

Optimism is the faith that leads to achievement. Nothing can be done without hope and confidence.

— *Helen Keller, writer and activist for the disabled*

Hope begins in the dark, the stubborn hope that if you just show up and try to do the right thing, the dawn will come. You wait and watch and work: You don't give up.

— *Anne Lamott, American writer*

Hope is the pillar that holds up the world. Hope is the dream of a waking man.

— *Pliny the Elder, 1st-century Roman naturalist*

Faith and doubt both are needed—not as antagonists, but working side by side to take us around the unknown curve.

— *Lillian Smith, American novelist and race activist*

Faith is not trying to believe something regardless of the evidence. Faith is daring to do something regardless of the consequences.

— *Sherwood Eddy, youth leader and YMCA activist*

If a man will begin in certainties he shall end in doubts; but if he will be content to begin in doubts he shall end in certainties.

— *Francis Bacon, 16th-century English essayist and statesman*

PART TWO:

the Body

* * *

There are few greater joys than the act of fully and completely digesting a good meal; what better place to contemplate this than in the toilet? A healthy bowel makes a happy man, and the quotations in this section offer some thoughts on health, the aging process, death and bodily decay, nature, gluttony, and vice. Writers and thinkers such as Gerard Manley Hopkins, Ambrose Bierce, Orson Welles, John Muir, Henry David Thoreau, Zora Neale Hurston, Benjamin Disraeli, Rumi, and Booker T. Washington also weigh in on the bathroom-bound concepts of relaxation, boredom, physical labor, clocks, breakfast, the belly, the delights of the natural world, and the pleasures of the bottle.

6. time and aging

Time grows dim. Time that was so long
Grows short, Time, all goggle-eyed,
Wiggling her skirts, singing her torch song,
Giving the boys a buzz and a ride,
That Nazi Mama with her beer and sauerkraut.
Time, old gal of mine, will soon dim out.

— *Anne Sexton, American poet*

To beguile the time,
Look like the time, bear welcome in your eye,
Your hand, your tongue; look like the innocent flower,
But be the serpent under't.

— *William Shakespeare, English playwright and poet*

Time is the substance from which I am made. Time is a river which
carries me along, but I am the river; it is a tiger that devours me, but
I am the tiger; it is a fire that consumes me, but I am the fire.

— *Jorge Luis Borges, Argentinean writer and poet*

No greater thing is created suddenly, any more than a bunch of grapes or a fig. If you tell me that you desire a fig, I answer you that there must be time. Let it first blossom, then bear fruit, then ripen.

— Epictetus, 2nd-century Roman Stoic and philosopher

Time stays long enough for anyone who will use it.

— Leonardo da Vinci, 15th-century painter, sculptor, and inventor

Time is the coin of your life. It is the only coin you have, and only you can determine how it will be spent. Be careful lest you let other people spend it for you.

— Carl Sandburg, American poet

Since time is not a person we can overtake when he is gone, let us honor him with mirth and cheerfulness of heart while he is passing.

— Johann Wolfgang von Goethe, German poet and novelist

We can chart our future clearly and wisely only when we know the path which has led to the present.

— Adlai Stevenson, American politician and vice president

Time, when it is left to itself and no definite demands are made on it, cannot be trusted to move at any recognized pace. Usually it loiters; but just when one has come to count upon its slowness, it may suddenly break into a wild irrational gallop.

> — *Edith Wharton, 19th-century American novelist*

I wasted time, and now doth time waste me.

> — *William Shakespeare, English playwright and poet*

Spend the afternoon. You can't take it with you.

> — *Annie Dillard, American essayist*

Time crumbles things; everything grows old under the power of time and is forgotten through the lapse of time.

> — *Aristotle, ancient Greek philosopher*

When you sit with a nice girl for two hours, it seems like two minutes; when you sit on a hot stove for two minutes, it seems like two hours. That's relativity.

> — *Albert Einstein, German-born American physicist*

How old would you be if you didn't know how old you are?

— *Satchel Paige, baseball pitcher*

Time is but the stream I go a-fishing in. I drink at it, but while I drink, I see the sandy bottom and detect how shallow it is. Its thin current slips away, but eternity remains.

— *Henry David Thoreau, Transcendentalist poet and writer*

Eternity is a mere moment, just long enough for a joke.

— *Hermann Hesse, German novelist*

The great French Marshall Lyautey once asked his gardener to plant a tree. The gardener objected that the tree was slow growing and would not reach maturity for 100 years. The Marshall replied, "In that case, there is no time to lose; plant it this afternoon!"

— *John F. Kennedy, American president and politician*

There is more time than life.

— *Mexican proverb*

Old age ain't no place for sissies.

— Bette Davis, American actress

Youth, which is forgiven everything, forgives itself nothing: age, which forgives itself everything, is forgiven nothing.

— George Bernard Shaw, Irish playwright and essayist

When I was young I was amazed at Plutarch's statement that the elder Cato began at the age of eighty to learn Greek. I am amazed no longer. Old age is ready to undertake tasks that youth shirked because they would take too long.

— W. Somerset Maugham, French-born novelist and playwright

Yesterday is gone. Tomorrow has not yet come. We have only today. Let us begin.

— Mother Teresa, Roman Catholic nun and missionary

Time: that which man is always trying to kill, ends in killing him.

— Herbert Spencer, 19th-century biologist and philosopher

But at my back I always hear
Time's winged chariot hurrying near;
And yonder all before us lie
Deserts of vast eternity.

— Andrew Marvell, 17th-century English poet

For age is opportunity no less
Than youth itself, though in another dress,
And as the evening twilight fades away,
The sky is filled with stars invisible by day.

— Henry Wadsworth Longfellow, 19th-century American poet

Grow old along with me!
The best is yet to be.
The last of life, for which the first was made.

— Robert Browning, 19th-century English poet

He who is of a calm and happy nature will hardly feel the pressure of age, but to him who is of an opposite disposition, youth and age are equally a burden.

— Plato, ancient Greek philosopher

I must govern the clock, not be governed by it.

> — *Golda Meir, Israeli prime minister*

Time, time, time, see what's become of me,
While I looked around, for my possibilities;
I was so hard to please.

> — *Paul Simon, American singer/songwriter*

There is nothing like returning to a place that remains unchanged to find the ways in which you yourself have altered.

> — *Nelson Mandela, South African statesman and president*

I never think of the future—it comes soon enough.

> — *Albert Einstein, German-born American physicist*

What can't be cured, must be endured.

> — *English proverb*

Real generosity toward the future lies in giving all to the present.

> — *Albert Camus, French novelist, playwright, and essayist*

Let any man examine his thoughts, and he will find them ever occupied with the past or the future. We scarcely think at all of the present; or if we do, it is only to borrow the light which it gives for regulating the future. The present is never our object; the past and the present we use as means; the future only is our end. Thus, we never live, we only hope to live.

— *Blaise Pascal, 17th-century French mathematician and theologian*

The sea does not reward those who are too anxious, too greedy, or too impatient. To dig for treasures shows not only impatience and greed, but lack of faith. Patience, patience, patience, is what the sea teaches. Patience and faith. One should lie empty, open, choiceless as a beach— waiting for a gift from the sea.

— *Anne Morrow Lindbergh, writer*

I think your whole life shows in your face and you should be proud of that.

— *Lauren Bacall, American film actress*

Life is a moderately good play with a badly written third act.

— *Truman Capote, American novelist*

A woman's always younger than a man of equal years.

> — *Elizabeth Barrett Browning, 19th-century English poet*

A comfortable old age is the reward of a well-spent youth. Instead of its bringing sad and melancholy prospects of decay, it would give us hopes of eternal youth in a better world.

> — *Maurice Chevalier, French vaudeville actor*

Old age, believe me, is a good and pleasant thing. It is true you are gently shouldered off the stage, but then you are given such a comfortable front stall as spectator.

> — *Confucius, ancient Chinese philosopher*

Youth is the best time to be rich, and the best time to be poor.

> — *Euripides, ancient Greek playwright and tragedian*

It was one of the deadliest and heaviest feelings of my life to feel that I was no longer a boy. From that moment I began to grow old in my own esteem—and in my esteem age is not estimable.

> — *Anatole France, 19th-century French writer*

Old age adds to the respect due to virtue, but it takes nothing from the contempt inspired by vice; it whitens only the hair.

— Ira Gershwin, American composer

When a noble life has prepared old age, it is not decline that it reveals, but the first days of immortality.

— Muriel Spark, British novelist

Time is really the only capital that any human being has, and the only thing he can't afford to lose.

— Thomas Edison, American inventor

The great use of life is to spend it on something that will outlast it.

— William James, 19th-century American philosopher

Try as they may to savor the taste of eternity, their thoughts still twist and turn upon the ebb and flow of things in past and future time. But if only their minds could be seized and held steady, they would be still for a while and, for that short moment, they would glimpse the splendor of eternity, which is forever still.

— St. Augustine of Hippo, 4th-century Church Father

The calendar is intolerable to all wisdom, the horror of all astronomy, and a laughing stock from a mathematician's point of view.

— *Roger Bacon, 13th-century scientist and philosopher*

The silent, never-resting thing called time, rolling, rushing on, swift, silent, like an all-embracing ocean tide... this is forever very literally a miracle; a thing to strike us dumb.

— *Thomas Carlyle, 19th-century Scottish scholar and writer*

Too slow for those who wait,
Too swift for those who fear,
Too long for those who grieve,
Too short for those who rejoice,
But for those who love,
Time is not.

— *Henry Jackson van Dyke, 19th-century American clergyman and writer*

As long as rivers shall run down to the sea, or shadows touch the mountain slopes, or stars graze in the vault of heaven, so long shall your honor, your name, your praises endure.

— *Virgil, 1st-century B.C. Latin poet*

Time is a cruel thief to rob us of our former selves. We lose as much to life as we do to death.

— *Elizabeth Forsythe Hailey, American feminist writer*

It is a mistake to regard age as a downhill grade toward dissolution. The reverse is true. As one grows older, one climbs with surprising strides.

— *George Sand, 19th-century French novelist*

Time will explain it all. He is a talker, and needs no questioning before he speaks.

— *Euripides, ancient Greek playwright and tragedian*

Live neither in the past nor in the future, but let each day's work absorb your entire energies, and satisfy your widest ambition.

— *William Ostler, 19th-century Canadian physician*

Look not mournfully into the past. It comes not back again. Wisely improve the present. It is thine. Go forth to meet the shadowy future, without fear.

— *Henry Wadsworth Longfellow, 19th-century American poet*

7. digestion and health

Health is my expected heaven.

— *John Keats, 19th-century English poet*

If God causes man to be sick, sickness must be good, and its opposite, health, must be evil, for all that He makes is good and will stand forever. If the transgression of God's law produces sickness, it is right to be sick; and we cannot if we would, and should not if we could, annul the decrees of wisdom.

— *Mary Baker Eddy, writer and founder of Christian Science*

But from the good health of the mind comes that which is dear to all and the object of prayer—happiness.

— *Aeschylus, ancient Greek playwright and tragedian*

Health, learning and virtue will ensure your happiness; they will give you a quiet conscience, private esteem and public honour.

— *Thomas Jefferson, American author and statesman*

Measure your health by your sympathy with morning and spring. If there is no response in you to the awakening of nature—if the prospect of an early morning walk does not banish sleep, if the warble of the first bluebird does not thrill you—know that the morning and spring of your life are past. Thus may you feel your pulse.

— *Henry David Thoreau, Transcendentalist poet and writer*

The preservation of health is a duty. Few seem conscious that there is such a thing as physical morality.

— *Herbert Spencer, 19th-century biologist and philosopher*

The true index of a man's character is the health of his wife.

— *Cyril Connolly, 20th-century English writer*

Man needs difficulties; they are necessary for health.

— *Carl Jung, Swiss psychiatrist*

Do not believe yourself healthy. Health will be immortality; this life is a long sickness.

— *St. Augustine of Hippo, 4th-century Church Father*

Health consists of having the same diseases as one's neighbors.

— *Quentin Crisp, English-born writer and performer*

Quit worrying about your health. It'll go away.

— *Robert Orben, American writer and editor*

Health nuts are going to feel stupid someday, lying in hospitals dying of nothing.

— *Redd Foxx, American comedian*

A man too busy to take care of his health is like a mechanic too busy to take care of his tools.

— *Spanish proverb*

Preserving health by too severe a rule is a worrisome malady.

— *Francois duc de la Rochefoucauld, 17th-century French writer*

A wise man should consider that health is the greatest of human blessings, and learn how by his own thought to derive benefit from his illnesses.

— *Hippocrates, 4th-century B.C. Greek physician*

Look to your health; and if you have it, praise God and value it next to conscience; for health is the second blessing that we mortals are capable of, a blessing money can't buy.

— Isaak Walton, 16th-century English writer and biographer

It is no measure of health to be well adjusted to a profoundly sick society.

— Jiddu Krishnamurti, 20th-century Indian philosopher

Nothing in Nature's sober found,
But an eternal health goes round.
Fill up the bowl, then, fill it high,
Fill all the glasses there—for why
Should every creature drink but I?
Why, man of morals, tell me why?

— Abraham Cowley, 17th-century English poet

Now good digestion wait on appetite,
And health on both!

— William Shakespeare, English playwright and poet

The problem with some people is that when they aren't drunk, they're sober.

— *W.B. Yeats, Irish poet*

First you take a drink, then the drink takes a drink, then the drink takes you.

— *F. Scott Fitzgerald, American novelist*

One cannot think well, love well, sleep well, if one has not dined well.

— *Virginia Woolf, English novelist*

Cooking is like love. It should be entered into with abandon or not at all.

— *Harriet Van Horne, American critic and columnist*

It is a hard matter, my fellow citizens, to argue with the belly, since it has no ears.

— *Plutarch, 1st-century historian and philosopher*

I no longer prepare food or drink with more than one ingredient.

— *Cyra McFadden, American essayist and novelist*

Never eat more than you can lift.

— *Miss Piggy, Jim Henson puppet*

Born to the earth are three kinds of creatures. Some are winged and fly. Some are furred and run. Still others stretch their mouths and talk. All must eat and drink to survive.

— *Lu Yu, 8th-century Chinese hermit and tea master*

A great step toward independence is a good-humored stomach.

— *Seneca, 1st-century Roman philosopher and statesman*

Food is the most primitive form of comfort.

— *Sheilah Graham, English-born Hollywood gossip columnist*

Everything ends this way in France. Weddings, christenings, duels, burials, swindlings, affairs of state—everything is a pretext for a good dinner.

— *Jean Anouilh, French playwright*

Eat breakfast like a king, lunch like a prince, and dinner like a pauper.

— *Adelle Davis, American nutritionist*

And malt does more than Milton can
To justify God's ways to man.
Ale, man, ale's the stuff to drink
For fellows whom it hurts to think.

— *A.E. Housman, English poet*

A man shouldn't fool with booze until he's fifty; then he's a damn fool if he doesn't.

— *William Faulkner, American novelist*

The smell of good bread baking, like the sound of lightly flowing water, is indescribable in its evocation of innocence and delight.

— *M.F.K. Fisher, American food writer*

We are all mortal until the first kiss and the second glass of wine.

— *Eduardo Galeano, Uruguayan writer and historian*

And now with some great pleasure I find that it's seven; and must cook dinner. Haddock and sausage meat. I think it is true that one gains a certain hold on haddock and sausage meat by writing them down.

— *Virginia Woolf, English novelist*

Two strong impulses: One
To drink long and deep,
the other,
not to sober up too soon.

— *Rumi, 13th-century Persian poet*

An alcoholic is someone you don't like who drinks as much as you do.

— *Dylan Thomas, Welsh poet*

All happiness depends on a leisurely breakfast.

— *John Gunther, American writer and journalist*

If more of us valued food and cheer and song above hoarded gold, it would be a merrier world.

— *J.R.R. Tolkien, British writer and scholar*

Candy
Is dandy
But liquor
Is quicker.

— *Ogden Nash, American humorist and poet*

There are people who strictly deprive themselves of each and every eatable, drinkable, and smokable which has in any way acquired a shady reputation. They pay this price for health. And health is all they get for it. How strange it is. It is like paying out your whole fortune for a cow that has gone dry.

— *Mark Twain, 19th-century American writer and humorist*

My doctor told me to stop having intimate dinners for four. Unless there are three other people.

— *Orson Welles, American actor and film director*

All human history attests
That happiness for man,—the hungry sinner!—
Since Eve ate apples, much depends on dinner.

— *Lord Byron, English Romantic poet*

Edible (adj). Good to eat and wholesome to digest, as a worm to a toad, a toad to a snake, a snake to a pig, a pig to a man, and a man to a worm.

— *Ambrose Bierce, American writer and journalist*

Digestion (n): The conversion of victuals into virtues.

— *Ambrose Bierce, American writer and journalist*

The wine urges me on, the bewitching wine, which sets even a wise man to singing and to laughing gently and rouses him up to dance and brings forth words which were better unspoken.

— Homer, ancient Greek poet

We are indeed much more than what we eat, but what we eat can nevertheless help us to be much more than what we are.

— Adelle Davis, American nutritionist

Preach not to others what they should eat, but eat as becomes you, and be silent.

— Epictetus, 2nd-century Roman stoic and philosopher

Make hunger thy sauce, as a medicine for health.

— Thomas Tusser, 16th-century English poet

The discovery of a new dish does more for human happiness than the discovery of a new star.

— Anthelme Brillat-Savarin, 18th-century French gastronome and writer

What is food to one, is to others bitter poison.

— *Lucretius, Roman poet and philosopher*

After a good dinner, one can forgive anybody, even one's relatives.

— *Oscar Wilde, 19th-century Irish poet and playwright*

Americans are just beginning to regard food the way the French always have. Dinner is not what you do in the evening before something else. Dinner is the evening.

— *Art Buchwald, American journalist*

Sir, respect your dinner: idolize it, enjoy it properly. You will be many hours in the week, many weeks in the year, and many years in your life happier if you do.

— *William Makepeace Thackeray, 19th-century British novelist*

My favorite animal is steak.

— *Fran Lebowitz, American humorist*

A man seldom thinks with more earnestness of anything than he does of his dinner.

— Samuel Johnson, 18th-century lexicographer and critic

A man's own dinner is to himself so important that he cannot bring himself to believe that it is a matter utterly indifferent to anyone else.

— Anthony Trollope, 19th-century English novelist

Ponder well on this point: The pleasant hours of our life are all connected by a more or less tangible link, with some memory of the table.

— Charles Pierre Monselet, 19th-century French writer

He may live without books—what is knowledge but grieving?
He may live without hope—what is hope but deceiving?
He may live without love—what is passion but pining?
But where is the man who can live without dining?

— Edward Bulwer-Lytton, 19th-century English poet and statesman

Digestion, of all the bodily functions, is the one which exercises the greatest influence on the mental state of an individual.

— Anthelme Brillat-Savarin, 18th-century French gastronome and writer

I prefer to regard a dessert as I would imagine the perfect woman: subtle, a little bittersweet, not blowsy and extrovert. Delicately made up, not highly rouged. Holding back, not exposing everything and, of course, with a flavor that lasts.

— *Graham Kerr, English chef and television personality*

If the divine creator has taken pains to give us delicious and exquisite things to eat, the least we can do is prepare them well and serve them with ceremony.

— *Fernand Point, French chef*

Part of the secret of success in life is to eat what you like and let the food fight it out inside.

— *Mark Twain, 19th-century American writer and humorist*

Dining is and always was a great artistic opportunity.

— *Frank Lloyd Wright, American architect*

Keen appetite
And quick digestion wait on you and yours.

— *John Dryden, 17th-century English poet*

8. work and leisure

The world is full of willing people, some willing to work, the rest
willing to let them.

> — *Robert Frost, American poet*

You are never given a wish without also being given the power to make
it true. You may have to work for it, however.

> — *Richard Bach, American writer and aviator*

Work is the grand cure of all the maladies and miseries that ever beset
mankind.

> — *Thomas Carlyle, 19th-century Scottish scholar and writer*

A wise man will make more opportunities than he finds.

> — *Francis Bacon, 16th-century English essayist and statesman*

It is one of the strange ironies of this strange life [that] those who work the hardest, who subject themselves to the strictest discipline, who give up certain pleasurable things in order to achieve a goal, are the happiest people.

— *Brutus Hamilton, Olympic pentathlete and coach*

No race can prosper till it learns there is as much dignity in tilling a field as in writing a poem.

— *Booker T. Washington, African-American educator and leader*

It is not only prayer that gives God glory but work. Smiting on an anvil, sawing a beam, whitewashing a wall, driving horses, sweeping, scouring, everything gives God some glory if being in his grace you do it as your duty.

— *Gerard Manley Hopkins, 19th-century English religious poet*

Work and struggle and never accept an evil that you can change.

— *Andre Gide, French writer and critic*

Satisfaction lies in the effort, not in the attainment; full effort is full victory.

— *Mohandas Gandhi, Indian statesman*

I believe that a person's true happiness comes from being able to look back in their past and feel they worked hard to achieve something and, in fact, achieved it.

— *Hirofumi Daimatsu, Japanese volleyball player and Olympic athlete*

The mode in which the inevitable comes to pass is through effort.

— *Oliver Wendell Holmes, American lawyer and judge*

I'm a great believer in luck, and I find the harder I work the more I have of it.

— *Thomas Jefferson, American author and statesman*

Opportunity is missed by most people because it comes dressed in overalls and looks like work.

— *Thomas Edison, American inventor*

It has been my experience that one cannot, in any shape or form, depend on human relations for lasting reward. It is only work that truly satisfies.

— *Bette Davis, American actress*

Measure not the work until the day's out and the labor done.

— *Elizabeth Barrett Browning, 19th-century English poet*

Hard work spotlights the character of people: Some turn up their sleeves, some turn up their noses, and some don't turn up at all.

— *Sam Ewing, American journalist and humorist*

Idleness and lack of occupation tend—nay are dragged—towards evil.

— *Hippocrates, 4th-century B.C. Greek physician*

Never be entirely idle; but either be reading, or writing, or praying or meditating or endeavoring something for the public good.

— *Thomas à Kempis, 15th-century German theologian*

Man is so made that he can only find relaxation from one kind of labor by taking up another.

— *Anatole France, 19th-century French writer*

Blessed is he who has found his work; let him ask no other blessedness.

— *Thomas Carlyle, 19th-century Scottish scholar and writer*

A human being must have occupation if he or she is not to become a nuisance to the world.

— *Dorothy L. Sayers, English writer of detective stories*

Derive happiness in oneself from a good day's work, from illuminating the fog that surrounds us.

— *Henri Matisse, French painter*

Life grants nothing to us mortals without hard work.

— *Horace, 1st-century B.C. Latin poet*

In order that people may be happy in their work, these three things are needed: They must be fit for it; They must not do too much of it; And they must have a sense of success in it.

— *John Ruskin, 19th-century English writer and art critic*

Never continue in a job you don't enjoy. If you're happy in what you're doing, you'll like yourself, you'll have inner peace. And if you have that, along with physical health, you will have had more success than you could possibly have imagined.

— *Johnny Carson, American comedian and television personality*

People who work sitting down get paid more than people who work standing up.

— Ogden Nash, American humorist and poet

The sweat of hard work is not to be displayed. It is much more graceful to appear favored by the gods.

— Maxine Hong Kingston, Asian-American writer and novelist

There is one piece of advice, in a life of study, which I think no one will object to; and that is, every now and then to be completely idle—to do nothing at all.

— Sydney Smith, 19th-century English essayist and humorist

Anyone can do any amount of work provided it isn't the work he is supposed to be doing at the moment.

— Robert Benchley, American humorist and magazine columnist

Far and away the best prize that life offers is the chance to work hard at work worth doing.

— Theodore Roosevelt, American politician and president

Cessation of work is not accompanied by cessation of expenses.

— *Cato the Elder, 3rd-century B.C. Roman statesman and prose writer*

Though ambition in itself is a vice, it often is also the parent of virtue.

— *Hosea Ballou, American Universalist clergyman and theologian*

All paid jobs absorb and degrade the mind.

— *Aristotle, ancient Greek philosopher*

Plans are only good intentions unless they immediately degenerate into hard work.

— *Peter Drucker, Austrian-born American businessman*

It is requisite for the relaxation of the mind that we make use, from time to time, of playful deeds and jokes.

— *St. Thomas Aquinas, 13th-century theologian*

I don't think necessity is the mother of invention—invention, in my opinion, arises directly from idleness, possibly also from laziness. To save oneself trouble.

— *Agatha Christie, English mystery novelist*

Ambition is a poor excuse for not having sense enough to be lazy.

— Edgar Bergen, American ventriloquist

Idleness is not doing nothing. Idleness is being free to do anything.

— Floyd Dell, American writer and socialist

Failure is not the only punishment for laziness; there is also the success of others.

— Jules Renard, French writer and memoirist

To be able to fill leisure intelligently is the last product of civilization, and at present very few people have reached this level.

— Bertrand Russell, British philosopher

Boredom is the feeling that everything is a waste of time; serenity, that nothing is.

— Thomas Szasz, Hungarian psychiatrist

If a man insisted always on being serious, and never allowed himself a bit of fun and relaxation, he would go mad or become unstable without knowing it.

— Herodotus, 5th-century B.C. Greek historian

Take rest; a field that has rested gives a bountiful crop.

— *Ovid, ancient Roman poet*

Far from idleness being the root of all evil, it is rather the only true good.

— *Soren Kierkegaard, 19th-century Danish philosopher and theologian*

One of the saddest things is that the only thing that a man can do for eight hours a day, day after day, is work. You can't eat eight hours a day nor drink for eight hours a day nor make love for eight hours—all you can do for eight hours is work. Which is the reason why man makes himself and everybody else so miserable and unhappy.

— *William Faulkner, American novelist*

It takes a lot of time to be a genius, you have to sit around so much doing nothing, really doing nothing.

— *Gertrude Stein, American writer*

It is already possible to imagine a society in which the majority of the population, that is to say, its laborers, will have almost as much leisure as in earlier times was enjoyed by the aristocracy. When one recalls how aristocracies in the past actually behaved, the prospect is not cheerful.

— *W.H. Auden, English poet*

Nothing brings more pain than too much pleasure; nothing brings more bondage than too much liberty.

> — *Benjamin Franklin, American writer, scientist, and statesman*

He has spent his life best who has enjoyed it most; God will take care that we do not enjoy it any more than is good for us.

> — *Samuel Butler, 17th-century English poet and satirist*

If you don't want to work you have to work to earn enough money so that you won't have to work.

> — *Ogden Nash, American humorist and poet*

I have discovered that all human evil comes from this, man's being unable to sit still in a room.

> — *Blaise Pascal, 17th-century French mathematician and theologian*

A man may be very industrious, and yet not spend his time well. There is no more fatal blunderer than he who consumes the greater part of life getting his living.

> — *Henry David Thoreau, Transcendentalist poet and writer*

Enjoy yourself. It's later than you think.

— Chinese proverb

Early to rise and early to bed makes a male healthy and wealthy and dead.

— James Thurber, American humorist

Laziness grows on people; it begins in cobwebs and ends in iron chains. The more one has to do, the more he is able to accomplish.

— Thomas Buxton, 19th-century English abolitionist and reformer

We are closer to the ants than to the butterflies. Very few people can endure much leisure.

— Gerald Brenan, travel writer

I can think of nothing less pleasurable than a life devoted to pleasure.

— John D. Rockefeller, Jr., American oil entrepreneur and philanthropist

Never be afraid to sit awhile and think.

— Lorraine Hansberry, African-American playwright

9. death and nature

Our fear of death is like our fear that summer will be short, but when we have had our swing of pleasure, our fill of fruit, and our swelter of heat we say we have had our day.

— *Ralph Waldo Emerson, 19th-century American author and activist*

We sometimes congratulate ourselves at the moment of waking from a troubled dream... it may be so at the moment of death.

— *Nathaniel Hawthorne, 19th-century American novelist*

Pale Death with impartial tread beats at the poor man's cottage door and at the palaces of kings.

— *Horace, 1st-century B.C. Latin poet*

For what is it to die, but to stand in the sun and melt into the wind? And when the Earth has claimed our limbs, then we shall truly dance.

— *Kahlil Gibran, Lebanese-born poet and novelist*

Is death the last sleep? No—it is the last and final awakening.

— *Sir Walter Scott, English poet and novelist*

If man hasn't discovered something that he will die for, he isn't fit to live.

— *Martin Luther King, Jr., Baptist minister and civil-rights leader*

Dying seems less sad than having lived too little.

— *Gloria Steinem, American writer and feminist activist*

Even death is unreliable: instead of zero it may be some ghastly
hallucination, such as the square root of minus one.

— *Samuel Beckett, Irish-born writer and playwright*

Death has got something to be said for it:
There's no need to get out of bed for it;
Wherever you may be,
They bring it to you, free.

— *Kingsley Amis, English novelist*

I want a busy life, a just mind, and a timely death.

— *Zora Neale Hurston, American novelist*

I shall die, but that is all that I shall do for Death; I am not on his payroll.

> — *Edna St. Vincent Millay, American poet*

I shall not die of a cold. I shall die of having lived.

> — *Willa Cather, 19th-century American novelist*

Goodbye, if you hear of my being stood up against a Mexican stone wall and shot to rags, please know that I think that a pretty good way to depart this life. It beats old age, disease, or falling down the cellar stairs. To be a Gringo in Mexico—ah, that is euthanasia!

> — *Ambrose Bierce, American writer and journalist*

We are spirits. That bodies should be lent us, while they can afford us pleasure, assist us in acquiring knowledge, or doing good to our fellow creatures, is a kind and benevolent act of God—when they become unfit for these purposes and afford us pain instead of pleasure... it is equally kind and benevolent that a way is provided by which we may get rid of them. Death is that way.

> — *Benjamin Franklin, American writer, scientist, and statesman*

The stars are the street lights of eternity.

> — *Rosicrucian proverb*

For certain is death for the born
And certain is birth for the dead;
Therefore over the inevitable
Thou shouldst not grieve.

— *The Bhagavad Gita*

Death is nothing to us, since when we are, death has not come, and when death has come, we are not.

— *Epicurus, 3rd-century Greek philosopher*

I said to Life, I would hear Death speak. And Life raised her voice a little higher and said, "You hear him now."

— *Kahlil Gibran, Lebanese-born poet and novelist*

As a well-spent day brings happy sleep, so life well used brings happy death.

— *Leonardo da Vinci, 15th-century painter, sculptor, and inventor*

It is impossible that anything so natural, so necessary, and so universal as death should ever have been designed by Providence as an evil to mankind.

— *Jonathan Swift, 18th-century Irish writer and satirist*

To fear death, my friends, is only to think ourselves wise, without being wise: for it is to think that we know what we do not know. For anything that men can tell, death may be the greatest good that can happen to them: but they fear it as if they knew quite well that it was the greatest of evils. And what is this but that shameful ignorance of thinking that we know what we do not know?

— Socrates, ancient Greek philosopher

If I had my life over again I should form the habit of nightly composing myself to thoughts of death. I would practice, as it were, the remembrance of death. There is no other practice which so intensifies life. Death, when it approaches, ought not to take one by surprise. It should be part of the full expectancy of life. Without an ever-present sense of death life is insipid. You might as well live on the whites of eggs.

— Muriel Spark, British novelist

Death is an endless night so awful to contemplate that it can make us love life and value it with such passion that it may be the ultimate cause of all joy and all art.

— Paul Theroux, American novelist and travel writer

The body is an instrument, the mind its function, the witness and reward of its operation.

— *George Santayana, Spanish-born American philosopher and critic*

It is the mind that makes the body.

— *Sojourner Truth, 19th-century American abolitionist and orator*

I am fearfully and wonderfully made.

— *Psalms 139:14*

One can say: "I will, but my body does not obey me"; but not: "My will does not obey me."

— *St. Augustine of Hippo, 4th-century Church Father*

The body is your instrument in dance, but your art is outside that creature, the body.

— *Martha Graham, American dancer and choreographer*

Our own physical body possesses a wisdom which we who inhabit the body lack. We give it orders which make no sense.

— *Henry Miller, American author and essayist*

Marriage, like death, is a debt we owe to nature.

— Julia Ward Howe, 19th-century American writer and reformer

We fancy that this din of religion, literature, and philosophy, which is heard in pulpits, lyceums, and parlors, vibrates through the universe, and is as catholic a sound as the creaking of the Earth's axle; but if a man sleeps soundly, he will forget it all between the sunset and dawn. It is the three-inch swing of a pendulum in a cupboard, which the great pulse of nature vibrates by and through each instant. When we lift our eyelids and open our ears, it disappears with smoke and rattle like the cars on a railroad. When I detect a beauty in any of the recesses of nature, I am reminded, by the serene and retired spirit in which it requires to be contemplated, of the inexpressible privacy of a life—how silent and unambitious it is.

— Henry David Thoreau, Transcendentalist poet and writer

I like trees because they seem more resigned to the way they have to live than other things do.

— Willa Cather, 19th-century American novelist

I only went out for a walk and finally concluded to stay out till sundown, for going out, I found, was really going in.

— John Muir, American naturalist and conservationist

No matter how often you knock at Nature's door, she won't answer in words you can understand—for Nature is dumb. She'll vibrate and moan like a violin, but you mustn't expect a song.

– Ivan Turgenev, 19th-century Russian novelist

Climb the mountains and get their good tidings. Nature's peace will flow into you as sunshine flows into trees. The winds will blow their own freshness into you, and the storms their energy, while cares will drop off like autumn leaves.

– John Muir, American naturalist and conservationist

What a book a devil's chaplain might write on the clumsy, wasteful, blundering, low, and horridly cruel works of nature!

– Charles Darwin, 19th-century naturalist and writer

If we think about it, we find that our life consists in a relation with all things: stone, earth, trees, flowers, water, insects, fishes, birds, creatures, sun, rainbow, children, women, other men. But his greatest and final relation is with the sun.

– D.H. Lawrence, English novelist and poet

The lowest and vilest alleys of London do not present a more dreadful record of sin than does the smiling and beautiful countryside.

— *Arthur Conan Doyle, Scottish writer and creator of Sherlock Holmes*

Nature has no mercy at all. Nature says, "I'm going to snow. If you have on a bikini and no snowshoes, that's tough. I am going to snow anyway."

— *Maya Angelou, American poet*

The loveliest of faces are to be seen by moonlight, when one sees half with the eye and half with the fancy.

— *Iranian proverb*

Every now and again take a good look at something not made with hands, a mountain, a star, the turn of a stream. There will come to you wisdom and patience and solace and, above all, the assurance that you are not alone in the world.

— *Sidney Lovett, writer and Yale University chaplain*

I am at two with nature.

— *Woody Allen, American film director and actor*

Accuse not Nature, she hath done her part; Do thou but thine.

— *John Milton, 17th-century English poet*

In all things of nature there is something of the marvelous.

— *Aristotle, ancient Greek philosopher*

A vacuum is a hell of a lot better than some of the stuff that nature replaces it with.

— *Tennessee Williams, American playwright*

The goal of life is living in agreement with nature.

— *Zeno of Citium, 3rd-century B.C. Greek philosopher and founder of the Stoic school*

Man has demonstrated that he is master of everything—except his own nature.

— *Henry Miller, American author and essayist*

Such is the audacity of man, that he hath learned to counterfeit Nature, yea, and is so bold as to challenge her in her work.

— *Pliny the Elder, 1st-century Roman naturalist*

Nature knows no pause in progress and development, and attaches her curse on all inaction.

— Johann Wolfgang von Goethe, German poet and novelist

Moonlight is sculpture.

— Nathaniel Hawthorne, 19th-century American novelist

Of all the things that oppress me, this sense of the evil working of nature herself—my disgust at her barbarity—clumsiness—darkness—bitter mockery of herself—is the most desolating.

— John Ruskin, 19th-century English writer and art critic

Nature, who for the perfect maintenance of the laws of her general equilibrium, has sometimes need of vices and sometimes of virtues, inspires now this impulse, now that one, in accordance with what she requires.

— Marquis de Sade, 18th-century French writer

The plastic virtues: purity, unity, and truth, keep nature in subjection.

— Guillaume Apollinaire, Italian-born French poet

To sit in the shade on a fine day, and look upon verdure is the most perfect refreshment.

— *Jane Austen, 19th-century English novelist*

In wilderness I sense the miracle of life, and behind it our scientific accomplishments fade to trivia.

— *Charles Lindbergh, American aviator*

10. sex and vice

The spirit is most often free when the body is satiated with pleasure; indeed, sometimes the stars shine more brightly seen from the gutter than from the hilltop.

— *W. Somerset Maugham, French-born novelist and playwright*

Sex is our deepest form of consciousness. It is utterly non-ideal, non-mental. It is pure blood-consciousness... It is the consciousness of the night, when the soul is almost asleep.

— *D.H. Lawrence, English novelist and poet*

Those who restrain desire, do so because theirs is weak enough to be restrained.

— *William Blake, 18th-century artist, poet, and mystic*

An untempted woman cannot boast of her chastity.

— *Michel de Montaigne, 16th-century French essayist*

Sins become more subtle as you grow older. You commit sins of despair rather than lust.

— Piers Paul Read, English novelist

Marriage is popular because it combines the maximum of temptation with the maximum of opportunity.

— George Bernard Shaw, Irish playwright and essayist

Sexual intercourse is kicking death in the ass while singing.

— Charles Bukowski, American novelist

If sex and creativity are often seen by dictators as subversive activities, it's because they lead to the knowledge that you own your own body (and with it your own voice), and that's the most revolutionary insight of all.

— Erica Jong, American writer

Electric flesh-arrows... traversing the body. A rainbow of color strikes the eyelids. A foam of music falls over the ears. It is the gong of the orgasm.

— Anais Nin, French-born writer and diarist

What pornography is really about, ultimately, isn't sex but death.

— *Susan Sontag, American essayist and critic*

Since we no longer write about a union with God, writing about sex has become the ultimate test for the writer: to communicate the incommunicable.

— *Michele Roberts, English feminist writer*

Sex is perhaps like culture—a luxury that only becomes an art after generations of leisurely acquaintance.

— *Alice B. Toklas, Lost Generation literary figure and cookbook author*

Everyone should study at least enough philosophy and belles lettres to make his sexual experience more delectable.

— *Georg Christoph Lichtenberg, 18th-century German educator, scientist, and writer*

Sex as an institution, sex as a general notion, sex as a problem, sex as a platitude—all this is something I find too tedious for words. Let's skip sex.

— *Vladimir Nabokov, Russian-born writer, poet, and critic*

I have always laid it down as a maxim—and found it justified by experience—that a man and a woman make far better friendships than can exist between two of the same sex—but then with the condition that they never have made or are to make love to each other.

— Lord Byron, English Romantic poet

It's not true the more sex that you have, the more it interferes with your work. I find that the more sex you have, the better work you do.

— H.G. Wells, English novelist and essayist

Lust is to the other passions what the nervous fluid is to life; it supports them all, lends strength to them all: Ambition, cruelty, avarice, revenge, are all founded on lust.

— Marquis de Sade, 18th-century French writer

Love is the answer—but while you're waiting for the answer sex raises some pretty good questions.

— Woody Allen, American film director and actor

When authorities warn you of the sinfulness of sex, there is an important lesson to be learned. Do not have sex with the authorities.

— Matt Groening, American cartoonist

A woman undressing, how dazzling. It is like the sun piercing the clouds.

— *August Rodin, 19th-century French sculptor*

You think it horrible that lust and rage
Should dance attendance upon my old age;
They were not such a plague when I was young;
What else have I to spur me into song?

— *W.B. Yeats, Irish poet*

He that but looketh on a plate of ham and eggs to lust after it, hath already committed breakfast with it in his heart.

— *C.S. Lewis, English novelist and critic*

Society drives people crazy with lust and calls it advertising.

— *John Lahr, American writer, drama critic, and biographer*

The weakest part of my body is a woman's eyes.

— *Anonymous*

Saintliness is also a temptation.

— *Jean Anouilh, French playwright*

For to tempt and to be tempted are things very nearly allied... whenever feeling has anything to do in the matter, no sooner is it excited than we have already gone vastly farther than we are aware of.

— *Catherine the Great, Catherine II of Russia*

Sex is the one thing you cannot really swindle; and it is the centre of the worst swindling of all, emotional swindling... Sex lashes out against counterfeit emotion, and is ruthless, devastating against false love.

— *D.H. Lawrence, English novelist and poet*

It is a monstrous thing that I will say, but I will say it all the same: I find in many things more restraint and order in my morals than in my opinions, and my lust less depraved than my reason.

— *Michel de Montaigne, 16th-century French essayist*

Morality in sexual situations, when it is free from superstition, consists essentially of respect for the other person, and unwillingness to use that person solely as a means of personal gratification, without regard to his or her desires.

— *Bertrand Russell, British philosopher*

Sex lies at the root of life, and we can never learn to reverence life until we know how to understand sex.

— *Havelock Ellis, English sexologist*

Our senses, our appetites, and our passions are our lawful and faithful guides in most things that relate solely to this life; and, therefore, by the hourly necessity of consulting them we gradually sink into an implicit submission, and habitual confidence. Every act of compliance with their motions facilitates a second compliance, every new step towards depravity is made with less reluctance than the former, and thus the descent to life merely sensual is accelerated.

— *Samuel Johnson, 18th-century lexicographer and critic*

How happy is the blameless vestal's lot? The world forgetting, by the world forgot.

— *Alexander Pope, 18th-century English poet*

The older one grows, the more one likes indecency.

— *Virginia Woolf, English novelist*

Lust is a mysterious wound in the side of humanity; or rather, at the very source of its life! To confound this lust in man with that desire which unites the sexes is like confusing a tumor with the very organ which it devours, a tumor whose very deformity horribly reproduces the shape.

— *Georges Bernanos, French religious writer*

Carnal lust rules where there is no love of God.

— *St. Augustine of Hippo, 4th-century Church Father*

One thing I've learned in all these years is not to make love when you really don't feel it; there's probably nothing worse you can do to yourself than that.

— *Norman Mailer, American writer*

Only a struggle twists sentimentality and lust together into love.

— *E.M. Forster, English novelist*

Alas, human vices, however horrible one might imagine them to be, contain the proof (were it only in their infinite expansion) of man's longing for the infinite; but it is a longing that often takes the wrong route. It is my belief that the reason behind all culpable excesses lies in this depravation of the sense of the infinite.

— *Charles Baudelaire, 19th-century French Symbolist poet*

Mortal lovers must not try to remain at the first step; for lasting passion is the dream of a harlot and from it we wake in despair.

— *C.S. Lewis, English novelist and critic*

Gluttony and Lust are the only sins that abuse something that is essential to our survival.

— *Henry Fairlie, political writer and biographer*

I wonder what fool it was that first invented kissing.

— *Jonathan Swift, 18th-century Irish writer and satirist*

What men call gallantry,
And gods adultery,
Is much more common
Where the climate's sultry.

— *Lord Byron, English Romantic poet*

If you live in rock and roll, as I do, you see the reality of sex, of male lust and women being aroused by male lust. It attracts women. It doesn't repel them.

— *Camille Paglia, American writer and critic*

It is no longer enough to be lusty. One must be a sexual gourmet.
— *George F. Will, American journalist and magazine columnist*

One can be a soldier without dying, and a lover without sighing.
— *Sir Edwin Arnold, 19th-century English poet*

The lover of life makes the whole world into his family, just as the lover of the fair sex creates his from all the lovely women he has found, from those that could be found, and those who are impossible to find.
— *Charles Baudelaire, 19th-century French Symbolist poet*

One who has not only the four S's, which are required in every good lover, but even the whole alphabet; as for example: Agreeable, Bountiful, Constant, Dutiful, Easy, Faithful, Gallant, Honorable, Ingenious, Kind, Loyal, Mild, Noble, Officious, Prudent, Quiet, Rich, Secret, True, Valiant, Wise; the X indeed, is too harsh a letter to agree with him, but he is Young and Zealous.
— *Miguel de Cervantes, 16th-century Spanish novelist and playwright*

Every man needs two women, a quiet homemaker, and a thrilling nymph.
— *Iris Murdoch, English novelist*

An orange on the table, your dress on the rug, and you in my bed, sweet present of the present, cool of night, warmth of my life.

— *Jacques Prévert, French Surrealist poet*

Busy old fool, unruly Sun, why dost thou thus through windows and through curtains call on us? Must to thy motions lovers seasons run?

— *John Donne, 16th-century metaphysical poet*

These two imparadised in one another's arms, the happier Eden, shall enjoy their fill of bliss on bliss.

— *John Milton, 17th-century English poet*

When a man and a woman have an overwhelming passion for each other, it seems to me, in spite of such obstacles dividing them as parents or husband, that they belong to each other in the name of Nature, and are lovers by Divine right, in spite of human convention or the laws.

— *Nicolas-Sebastien Chamfort, 18th-century French writer and humorist*

No one worth possessing can be quite possessed.

— *Sara Teasdale, American poet*

PART THREE:

the Mind

* * *

Augustus Caesar said that well done is quickly done, which may be true in battle but in the bathroom, haste can only make waste. The key to a well-spent, satisfying bathroom break is a slow and steady pace, together with a sense of peace and absolute privacy. The passages in this chapter discuss the psychology of privacy, solitude, and loneliness, as well as the tensions and demands of society and social interaction. Also addressed are the virtues of patience and humility, both handy to have around when in the toilet, as well as other issues of the intellect, such as morality, defeat, rejection, perseverance, honor, ambition, and conscience. Writers such as Robert Louis Stevenson, Thomas Aquinas, Ayn Rand, Ralph Waldo Emerson, and Aristotle also contemplate the issues surrounding modesty, failure, unconventionality, gossip, strength of character, pride, sin, the nature of evil, the purpose of art, the joys and pains of the creative mind, and the true meaning of success.

11. adversity and success

If you're going through hell, keep going.

— *Winston Churchill, British statesman and prime minister*

I have been in Sorrow's kitchen and licked out all the pots. Then I have stood on the peaky mountain wrapped in rainbows, with a harp and a sword in my hands.

— *Zora Neale Hurston, American novelist*

For the man sound in body and serene in mind there is no such thing as bad weather; every sky has its beauty, and storms which whip the blood do but make it pulse more vigorously.

— *Jerome K. Jerome, English humorist and writer*

You may encounter many defeats, but you must not be defeated. In fact, it may be necessary to encounter the defeats, so you can know who you are, what you can rise from, how you can still come out of it.

— *Maya Angelou, American poet*

If we had no winter, the spring would not be so pleasant; if we did not sometimes taste of adversity, prosperity would not be so welcome.

— *Anne Bradstreet, 17th-century English poet*

Life is truly known only to those who suffer, lose, endure adversity and stumble from defeat to defeat.

— *Anais Nin, French-born writer and diarist*

Difficulties strengthen the mind, as labor does the body.

— *Seneca, 1st-century Roman philosopher and statesman*

Life affords no higher pleasure than that of surmounting difficulties, passing from one step of success to another, forming new wishes, and seeing them gratified. He that labors in any great or laudable undertaking has his fatigues first supported by hope, and afterwards rewarded by joy.

— *Samuel Johnson, 18th-century lexicographer and critic*

Behold, I have refined thee, but not with silver; I have chosen thee in the furnace of affliction.

— *Isaiah 48:10*

Adversity is the trial of principle. Without it man hardly knows whether he is honest or not.

— *Henry Fielding, 18th-century English playwright and novelist*

Prosperity doth best discover vice; but adversity doth best discover virtue.

— *Francis Bacon, 16th-century English essayist and statesman*

If you break your neck, if you have nothing to eat, if your house is on fire, then you got a problem. Everything else is inconvenience.

— *Robert Fulghum, American self-help writer*

Sometimes it's worse to win a fight than to lose.

— *Billie Holiday, American jazz vocalist*

Don't be discouraged by a failure. It can be a positive experience. Failure is, in a sense, the highway to success, inasmuch as every discovery of what is false leads us to seek earnestly after what is true, and every fresh experience points out some form of error which we shall afterwards carefully avoid.

— *John Keats, 19th-century English poet*

A slave is one who waits for someone to come and free him.

— Ezra Pound, American poet

If a thing is worth doing, it is worth doing badly.

— G.K. Chesterton, English essayist and author

Better to light a candle than to curse the darkness.

— Chinese proverb

Every strike brings me closer to the next home run.

— Babe Ruth, baseball player

I have not failed. I've just found 10,000 ways that won't work.

— Thomas Edison, American inventor

If you wish success in life, make perseverance your bosom friend, experience your wise counselor, caution your elder brother and hope your guardian genius.

— Joseph Addison, 17th-century English essayist

Our errors are surely not such awfully solemn things. In a world where we are so certain to incur them in spite of all our caution, a certain lightness of heart seems healthier than this excessive nervousness on their behalf.

— *William James, 19th-century American philosopher*

To laugh often and much; to win the respect of intelligent people and the affection of children; to earn the appreciation of honest critics and endure the betrayal of false friends; to appreciate beauty, to find the best in others; to leave the world a little better; whether by a healthy child, a garden patch or a redeemed social condition; to know even one life has breathed easier because you have lived. This is the meaning of success.

— *Ralph Waldo Emerson, 19th-century American author and activist*

Ah but a man's reach should exceed his grasp, or what's a heaven for?

— *Robert Browning, 19th-century English poet*

The outer limit of your potential is determined solely by your own beliefs and your own confidence in what you think is possible.

— *Brian Tracy, American businessman and motivational speaker*

Men are anxious to improve their circumstances, but are unwilling to improve themselves; they therefore remain bound.

— James Allen, 19th-century American novelist

Each human being is bred with a unique set of potentials that yearn to be fulfilled as surely as the acorn yearns to become the oak within it.

— Aristotle, ancient Greek philosopher

Most people would succeed in small things if they were not troubled with great ambitions.

— Henry Wadsworth Longfellow, 19th-century American poet

A life spent making mistakes is not only more honorable, but more useful than a life spent doing nothing.

— George Bernard Shaw, Irish playwright and essayist

The beauty of the world has two edges, one of laughter, one of anguish, cutting the heart asunder.

— Virginia Woolf, English novelist

Success usually comes to those who are too busy to be looking for it.

— Henry David Thoreau, Transcendentalist poet and writer

The moral flabbiness born of the exclusive worship of the Bitch-Goddess success. That—with the squalid cash interpretation put on the word success—is our national disease.

— William James, 19th-century American philosopher

Success consists of going from failure to failure without loss of enthusiasm.

— Winston Churchill, British statesman and prime minister

A failure is a man who has blundered, but is not able to cash in on the experience.

— Elbert Hubbard, 19th-century writer, educator, and member of the Arts and Crafts movement

Aim at heaven and you will get earth thrown in. Aim at earth and you get neither.

— C.S. Lewis, English novelist and critic

Not failure, but low aim, is crime.

> — *James Russell Lowell, 19th-century American poet and magazine editor*

The past is our definition. We may strive, with good reason, to escape it, or to escape what is bad in it, but we will escape it only by adding something better to it.

> — *Wendell Berry, American poet and essayist*

We must be willing to get rid of the life we've planned, so as to have the life that is waiting for us.

> — *Joseph Campbell, American mythologist and educator*

She had an unequalled gift... of squeezing big mistakes into small opportunities.

> — *Henry James, American novelist*

We succeed only as we identify in life, or in war, or in anything else, a single overriding objective, and make all other considerations bend to that one objective.

> — *Dwight D. Eisenhower, American president and military commander*

Alas, we make a ladder of our thoughts, where angels step, but sleep ourselves at the foot; our high resolves look down upon our slumbering acts.

— Letitia E. Landon, 19th-century English poet and critic

Of course there is no formula for success except perhaps an unconditional acceptance of life and what it brings.

— Arthur Rubinstein, Polish-born pianist

Good people are good because they've come to wisdom through failure.

— William Saroyan, American writer and playwright

This thing that we call "failure" is not the falling down, but the staying down.

— Mary Pickford, Canadian-born film actress

A minute's success pays the failure of years.

— Robert Browning, 19th-century English poet

Why be a man when you can be a success?

— Bertolt Brecht, German playwright

A man's life is interesting primarily when he has failed—I well know.
For it's a sign that he tried to surpass himself.

> — *Georges Clemenceau, French politician and prime minister*

You owe it to us all to get on with what you're good at.

> — *W.H. Auden, English poet*

Many of life's failures are people who did not realize how close they
were to success when they gave up.

> — *Thomas Edison, American inventor*

Whatever you are by nature, keep to it; never desert your line of talent.
Be what nature intended you for and you will succeed.

> — *Sydney Smith, 19th-century English essayist and humorist*

There is only one success—to be able to spend your life in your own way.

> — *Christopher Morley, American novelist and essayist*

The life of every man is a diary in which he means to write one story,
and writes another.

> — *J.M. Barrie, Scottish playwright and author*

Seize opportunity by the beard, for it is bald behind.

— Bulgarian proverb

Small opportunities are often the beginning of great enterprises.

— Demosthenes, 4th-century B.C. Greek orator

Formulate and stamp indelibly on your mind a mental picture of yourself as succeeding. Hold this picture tenaciously. Never permit it to fade. Your mind will seek to develop the picture. Do not build up obstacles in your imagination.

— Norman Vincent Peale, American religious writer

Failure is the condiment that gives success its flavor.

— Truman Capote, American novelist

12. solitude and society

Be not conformed to this world.

— *Romans 12:2*

Loneliness is the poverty of self; solitude is the richness of self.

— *May Sarton, Belgian-born American poet and educator*

Do not allow yourself to be imprisoned by any affection. Keep your solitude. The day, if it ever comes, when you are given true affection, there will be no opposition between interior solitude and friendship, quite the reverse. It is even by this infallible sign that you will recognize it.

— *Simone Weil, French philosopher*

The thing that makes you exceptional, if you are at all, is inevitably that which must also make you lonely.

— *Lorraine Hansberry, American playwright*

You do not need to leave your room. Remain sitting at your table and listen. Do not even listen, simply wait. Do not even wait, be quiet, still and solitary. The world will freely offer itself to you to be unmasked, it has no choice, it will roll in ecstasy at your feet.

— *Franz Kafka, Czech writer*

We allow our ignorance to prevail upon us and make us think we can survive alone, alone in patches, alone in groups, alone in races, even alone in genders.

— *Maya Angelou, American poet*

Social opinion is like a sharp knife. There are foolish people who regard it only with terror, and dare not touch or meddle with it; there are more foolish people, who, in rashness or defiance, seize it by the blade, and get cut and mangled for their pains; and there are wise people, who grasp it discreetly and boldly by the handle and use it to carve out their own purposes.

— *Anna Jameson, 19th-century Irish novelist and travel writer*

Solitude is un-American.

— *Erica Jong, American writer*

One of the greatest necessities in America is to discover creative solitude.

— *Carl Sandburg, American poet*

When they are alone they want to be with others, and when they are with others they want to be alone. After all, human beings are like that.

— *Gertrude Stein, American writer*

Being an old maid is like death by drowning—really a delightful sensation after you have ceased struggling.

— *Edna Ferber, American writer and essayist*

She was not accustomed to taste the joys of solitude except in company.

— *Edith Wharton, 19th-century American novelist*

She would never exchange her solitude for anything. Never again to be forced to move to the rhythms of others.

— *Tillie Olson, American social critic and short-story writer*

On the outskirts of every agony sits some observant fellow who points.

— *Virginia Woolf, English novelist*

We're born alone, we live alone, we die alone. Only through our love and friendship can we create the illusion for the moment that we're not alone.

— *Orson Welles, American actor and film director*

Solitude is the profoundest fact of the human condition. Man is the only being who knows he is alone.

— *Octavio Paz, Mexican poet*

Solitude is as needful to the imagination as society is wholesome for the character.

— *James Russell Lowell, 19th-century poet and magazine editor*

When you close your doors, and make darkness within, remember never to say that you are alone, for you are not alone; nay, God is within, and your genius is within. And what need have they of light to see what you are doing?

— *Epictetus, 2nd-century Roman stoic and philosopher*

Isolation is the sum total of wretchedness to a man.

— *Thomas Carlyle, 19th-century Scottish scholar and writer*

A lonely man is a lonesome thing, a stone, a bone, a stick, a receptacle for Gilbey's gin, a stooped figure sitting at the edge of a hotel bed, heaving copious sighs like the autumn wind.

— *John Cheever, American novelist and short-story writer*

Who knows what true loneliness is—not the conventional word, but the naked terror? To the lonely themselves it wears a mask. The most miserable outcast hugs some memory or some illusion. Now and then a fatal conjunction of events may lift the veil for an instant. For an instant only. No human being could bear a steady view of moral solitude without going mad.

— *Joseph Conrad, Polish-born novelist*

There's nothing like eavesdropping to show you that the world outside your head is different from the world inside your head.

— *Thornton Wilder, American novelist and playwright*

That which happens to soil when it ceases to be cultivated, happens to man himself when he foolishly forsakes society for solitude; the brambles grow up in his desert heart.

— *Antoine Rivarol, 18th-century French journalist and monarchist*

Not only does democracy make every man forget his ancestors, but also clouds their view of their descendants and isolates them from their contemporaries. Each man is forever thrown back on himself alone, and there is danger that he may be shut up in the solitude of his own heart.

— *Alexis de Tocqueville, French historian and political scientist*

The whole business of your life overwhelms you when you live alone. One's stupefied by it. To get rid of it you try to daub some of it off on to people who come to see you, and they hate that. To be alone trains one for death.

— *Louis-Ferdinand Celine, French writer and physician*

Oh to have a lodge in some vast wilderness. Where rumors of oppression and deceit, of unsuccessful and successful wars may never reach me anymore.

— *William Cowper, 18th-century English poet*

True solitude is a din of birdsong, seething leaves, whirling colors, or a clamor of tracks in the snow.

— *Edward Hoagland, American novelist and educator*

At his best, man is the noblest of all animals; separated from law and justice he is the worst.

— *Aristotle, ancient Greek philosopher*

Underlying the whole scheme of civilization is the confidence men have in each other, confidence in their integrity, confidence in their honesty, confidence in their future.

— *Bourke Cockran, 19th-century Irish-American politician*

Live in such a way that you would not be ashamed to sell your parrot to the town gossip.

— *Will Rogers, radio and stage actor*

Nothing is as peevish and pedantic as men's judgments of one another.

— *Desiderius Erasmus, Dutch writer and Humanist*

Be kind, for everyone you meet is fighting a harder battle.

— *Plato, ancient Greek philosopher*

We are each other's harvest; we are each other's business; we are each other's magnitude and bond.

— Gwendolyn Brooks, African-American poet

The first duty of a human being is to assume the right relationship to society—more briefly, to find your real job, and do it.

— Charlotte Perkins Gilman, American writer, editor, and reformer

Men have been taught that it is a virtue to agree with others. But the creator is the man who disagrees. Men have been taught that it is a virtue to swim with the current. But the creator is the man who goes against the current. Men have been taught that it is a virtue to stand together. But the creator is the man who stands alone.

— Ayn Rand, Russian-born novelist and philosopher

Keep a diary and one day it'll keep you.

— Mae West, American film actress

The love of our neighbor in all its fullness simply means being able to say, "What are you going through?"

— Simone Weil, French philosopher

It is good to rub and polish our brain against that of others.

— Michel de Montaigne, 16th-century French essayist

To succeed in the world it is not enough to be stupid, you must also be well-mannered.

— Voltaire, French Enlightenment writer

Society is like the air, necessary to breathe but insufficient to live on.

— George Santayana, Spanish-born American philosopher and critic

A noble heart never forces itself forward—its words are as rare gems, seldom displayed and of great value.

— Zen proverb

As iron is eaten away by rust, so the envious are consumed by their own passion.

— Antisthenes, Greek philosopher and cofounder of the Cynic school

To live alone is the fate of all great souls.

— Arthur Schopenhauer, Polish-born 19th-century philosopher

Genius is eternal patience.

> — *Michelangelo, 16th-century Florentine painter and sculptor*

Tact is the ability to describe others as they see themselves.

> — *Abraham Lincoln, American president and lawyer*

Many a man's reputation would not know his character if they met on the street.

> — *Elbert Hubbard, 19th-century writer, educator,*
> *and member of the Arts and Crafts movement*

Most lives are spent putting on and taking off masks.

> — *Gore Vidal, American writer and critic*

Should they whisper false of you,
Never trouble to deny;
Should the words they say be true,
Weep and storm and swear they lie.

> — *Dorothy Parker, American poet and humorist*

To be social is to be forgiving.

— *Robert Frost, American poet*

I have never made but one prayer to God, a very short one: O Lord, make my enemies ridiculous. And God granted it.

— *Voltaire, French Enlightenment writer*

One may have a blazing hearth in one's soul and yet no one ever comes to sit by it. Passersby see only a wisp of smoke from the chimney and continue on the way.

— *Vincent van Gogh, Dutch painter*

Society is now one polished horde,
Formed of two mighty tribes,
The Bores and the Bored.

— *Lord Byron, English Romantic poet*

13. patience and humility

Natural heart's ivy, Patience masks
Our ruins of wrecked past purpose.

> — *Gerard Manley Hopkins, 19th-century English religious poet*

Patience, that blending of moral courage with physical timidity.

> — *Thomas Hardy, English novelist*

With patience bear what pains you have deserved,
Grieve, if you will, over what's unmerited.

> — *Ovid, ancient Roman poet*

Experience, like a pale musician, holds
A dulcimer of patience in his hand.

> — *Elizabeth Barrett Browning, 19th-century English poet*

Genius is eternal patience.

> — *Michelangelo, 16th-century Florentine painter and sculptor*

Remember that you are an actor in a drama, of such a part as it may please the master to assign you, for a long time or for a little as he may choose. And if he will you to take the part of a poor man, or a cripple, or a ruler, or a private citizen, then may you act that part with grace! For to act well the part that is allotted to us, that indeed is ours to do, but to choose it is another's.

— *Epictetus, 2nd-century Roman stoic and philosopher*

It takes patience to appreciate domestic bliss; volatile spirits prefer unhappiness.

— *George Santayana, Spanish-born American philosopher and critic*

Perhaps there is only one cardinal sin: impatience. Because of impatience we were driven out of Paradise, because of impatience we cannot return.

— *W.H. Auden, English poet*

Beware the fury of a patient man.

— *John Dryden, 17th-century English poet*

The fates have given mankind a patient soul.

— *Homer, ancient Greek poet*

Sense shines with a double luster when it is set in humility. An able yet humble man is a jewel worth a kingdom.

> — *William Penn, 17th-century religious leader and American colonist*

All things pass… patience attains all it strives for.

> — *Mother Teresa, Roman Catholic nun and missionary*

Endurance is the crowning quality,
And patience all the passion of great hearts.

> — *James Russell Lowell, 19th-century poet and magazine editor*

Never think that God's delays are God's denials. Hold on; hold fast; hold out. Patience is genius.

> — *George-Louis Leclerc du Buffon, 18th-century French naturalist*

Patience serves as a protection against wrongs as clothes do against cold. For if you put on more clothes as the cold increases, it will have no power to hurt you. So in like manner you must grow in patience when you meet with great wrongs, and they will then be powerless to vex your mind.

> — *Leonardo da Vinci, 15th-century painter, sculptor, and inventor*

Patience and delay achieve more than force and rage.

— *Jean de La Fontaine, 17th-century French poet and classicist*

Perfection is achieved, not when there is nothing more to add, but when there is nothing left to take away.

— *Antoine de Saint-Exupery, French writer*

Have patience with all things, but chiefly have patience with yourself. Do not lose courage in considering your own imperfections but instantly set about remedying them—every day begin the task anew.

— *St. Francis of Sales, 16th-century Roman Catholic bishop*

Have courage for the great sorrows of life and patience for the small ones; and when you have laboriously accomplished your daily task, go to sleep in peace. God is awake.

— *Victor Hugo, 19th-century French poet and novelist*

The greatest of faults, I should say, is to be conscious of none.

— *Thomas Carlyle, 19th-century Scottish scholar and writer*

A mule will labor ten years willingly and patiently for you, for the privilege of kicking you once.

> — *William Faulkner, American novelist*

Only those who have the patience to do simple things perfectly will acquire the skill to do difficult things easily.

> — *Friedrich Schiller, 18th-century German poet and historian*

As blushing will sometimes make a whore pass for a virtuous woman, so modesty may make a fool seem a man of sense.

> — *Jonathan Swift, 18th-century Irish writer and satirist*

God has two dwellings: one in heaven, and the other in a meek and thankful heart.

> — *Isaak Walton, 16th-century English writer and biographer*

It is by attempting to reach the top in a single leap that so much misery is produced in the world.

> — *William Cobbett, 19th-century English reformer, journalist, and educator*

Manifest plainness,
Embrace simplicity,
Reduce selfishness,
Have few desires.

— Lao-tzu, 6th-century B.C. founder of Chinese Taoism

Only those who feel little in the eyes of God, can hope to be mighty in the eyes of men.

— Ernest Moritz Arndt, 19th-century German poet

It is no great thing to be humble when you are brought low; but to be humble when you are praised is a great and rare attainment.

— St. Bernard, 12th-century French churchman

Those who are believed to be most abject and humble are usually most ambitious and envious.

— Baruch Spinoza, 17th-century Dutch philosopher and theologian

I was born modest; not all over, but in spots.

— Mark Twain, 19th-century American writer and humorist

I believe that the first test of a truly great man is his humility. I don't mean by humility, doubt of his power. But really great men have a curious feeling that the greatness is not of them, but through them. And they see something divine in every other man and are endlessly, foolishly, incredibly merciful.

— *John Ruskin, 19th-century English writer and art critic*

Humility is a virtue all preach, none practice, and yet everybody is content to hear. The master thinks it good doctrine for his servant, the laity for the clergy, and the clergy for the laity.

— *John Selden, 17th-century English historian*

Discourses on humility are a source of pride in the vain and of humility in the humble. So those on skepticism cause believers to affirm. Few men speak humbly of humility, chastely of chastity, few doubtingly of skepticism.

— *Blaise Pascal, 17th-century French mathematician and theologian*

A man who has humility will have acquired in the last reaches of his beliefs the saving doubt of his own certainty.

— *Walter Lippmann, American political writer*

Humility has its origin in an awareness of unworthiness, and sometimes too in a dazzled awareness of saintliness.

— Colette, French novelist

And the Devil did grin, for his darling sin
Is pride that apes humility.

— Samuel Taylor Coleridge, English poet

No place affords a more striking conviction of the vanity of human hopes than a public library; for who can see the wall crowded on every side by mighty volumes, the works of laborious meditations and accurate inquiry, now scarcely known but by the catalogue.

— Samuel Johnson, 18th-century lexicographer and critic

Be nice to people on your way up because you may meet them again on your way down.

— Jimmy Durante, American comedian

The sun will set without your assistance.

— The Talmud

If I only had a little humility, I'd be perfect.

> — *Ted Turner, American media businessman*

Always acknowledge a fault. This will throw those in authority off their guard and give you an opportunity to commit more.

> — *Mark Twain, 19th-century American writer and humorist*

Whenever I see an erring man, I say to myself, I have also erred. When I see a lustful man I say to myself, so was I once. And in this way I feel kinship with everyone in the world and feel that I cannot be happy without the humblest of us being happy.

> — *Mohandas Gandhi, Indian statesman*

Someone's boring me. I think it's me.

> — *Dylan Thomas, Welsh poet*

"I have done that," says my memory. "I cannot have done that," says my pride, and remains inexorable. Eventually—memory yields.

> — *Friedrich Nietzsche, 19th-century German philosopher*

Pride, perceiving humility honorable, often borrows her cloak.

— *Thomas Fuller, 17th-century English clergyman and humorist*

Humility is no substitute for personality.

— *Fran Lebowitz, American humorist*

Humility provides everyone, even him who despairs in solitude, with the strongest relationship to his fellow man, and this immediately, though, of course, only in the case of complete and permanent humility.

— *Franz Kafka, Czech writer*

Pride is the mask of one's own faults.

— *Jewish proverb*

It is the duty of the human understanding to understand that there are things which it cannot understand, and what those things are. Human understanding has vulgarly occupied itself with nothing but understanding, but if it would only take the trouble to understand itself at the same time it would simply have to posit the paradox.

— *Soren Kierkegaard, 19th-century Danish philosopher and theologian*

I long to accomplish great and noble tasks, but it is my chief duty to accomplish humble tasks as though they were great and noble. The world is moved along, not only by the mighty shoves of its heroes, but also by the aggregate of the tiny pushes of each honest worker.

— *Helen Keller, writer and activist for the disabled*

There are two main human sins from which all the others derive: impatience and indolence. It was because of impatience that they were expelled from Paradise, it is because of indolence that they do not return. Yet perhaps there is only one major sin: impatience. Because of impatience they were expelled, because of impatience they do not return.

— *Franz Kafka, Czech writer*

A man in the view of absolute goodness adores with total humility. Every step downward, is a step upward. The man who renounces himself, comes to himself.

— *Ralph Waldo Emerson, 19th-century American author and activist*

Arrogance invites ruin; humility receives benefits.

— *Chinese proverb*

Pride asserts, humility testifies. The proud want to seem what they are not. The one who gives testimony does not want to appear what he is not but to love what, in the full sense, is.

— *St. Augustine of Hippo, 4th-century Church Father*

14. weakness and morality

Shame arises from the fear of man; conscience from the fear of God.

— *Samuel Johnson, 18th-century lexicographer and critic*

He who reigns within himself and rules his passions, desires, and fears is more than a king.

— *John Milton, 17th-century English poet*

I love the man that can smile in trouble, that can gather strength from distress, and grow brave by reflection. 'Tis the business of little minds to shrink, but he whose heart is firm, and whose conscience approves his conduct, will pursue his principles unto death.

— *Thomas Paine, 18th-century American political scientist and writer*

To educate a man in mind and not in morals is to educate a menace to society.

— *Theodore Roosevelt, American politician and president*

When man has neither the strength to subdue his underworld powers—which are really the ancient powers of his old, superseded self; nor the wit to placate them with sacrifice and the burnt holocaust; then they come back at him, and destroy him again. Hence every new conquest of life means a "harrowing of Hell."

— *D.H. Lawrence, English novelist and poet*

Keep your fears to yourself, but share your courage with others.

— *Robert Louis Stevenson, 19th-century Scottish author*

Evil denotes the lack of good. Not every absence of good is an evil, for absence may be taken either in a purely negative or in a private sense. Mere negation does not display the character of evil, otherwise nonexistence would be evil and moreover, a thing would be evil for not possessing the goodness of something else, which would mean that man is bad for not having the strength of a lion or the speed of a wild goat. But what is evil is privation; in this sense blindness means the privation of sight.

— *St. Thomas Aquinas, 13th-century theologian*

Character is what you are in the dark.

— *Dwight L. Moody, 19th-century Protestant preacher*

Be of good cheer about death and know this as a truth—that no evil can happen to a good man, either in life or after death.

— *Socrates, ancient Greek philosopher*

But Satan now is wiser than of yore, and tempts by making rich, not making poor.

— *Alexander Pope, 18th-century English poet*

If weakness may excuse, what Murderer, what Traitor, Parricide, Incestuous, Sacrilegious, but may plead it? All Wickedness is Weakness: that plea therefore with God or Man will gain thee no Remission.

— *John Milton, 17th-century English poet*

Morality is of the highest importance—but for us, not for God.

— *Albert Einstein, German-born American physicist*

It is a talent of the weak to persuade themselves that they suffer for something when they suffer from something; that they are showing the way when they are running away; that they see the light when they feel the heat; that they are chosen when they are shunned.

— *Eric Hoffer, American philosopher*

The true meaning of religion is thus, not simply morality, but morality touched by emotion.

— Matthew Arnold, 19th-century English poet

Out of the mouths of babes and sucklings hast thou ordained strength.

— Matthew 25:29

There is nothing in which people more betray their character than in what they laugh at.

— Johann Wolfgang von Goethe, German poet and novelist

Strengthen me by sympathizing with my strength, not my weakness.

— Bronson Alcott, 19th-century Transcendentalist educator and reformer

Conscience is a mother-in-law whose visit never ends.

— H.L. Mencken, American journalist and essayist

The wise man in the storm prays to God, not for safety from danger, but for deliverance from fear.

— Ralph Waldo Emerson, 19th-century American author and activist

Do you really think it is weakness that yields to temptation? I tell you that there are terrible temptations which it requires strength, strength and courage to yield to.

— *Oscar Wilde, 19th-century Irish poet and playwright*

A woman is like a tea bag—only in hot water do you realize how strong she is.

— *Nancy Reagan, screen actress and American first lady*

God be kind to all good Samaritans and also the bad ones. For such is the kingdom of heaven.

— *John Gardner, American novelist*

Our goodness comes solely from thinking on goodness; our wickedness from thinking on wickedness. We too are the victims of our own contemplation.

— *John Jay Chapman, American poet and critic*

Abstainer: A weak man who yields to the temptation of denying himself a pleasure.

— *Ambrose Bierce, American writer and journalist*

Give me the benefit of your convictions, if you have any, but keep your doubts to yourself, for I have enough of my own.

— Johann Wolfgang von Goethe, German poet and novelist

In the ocean of baseness, the deeper we get, the easier the sinking.

— James Russell Lowell, 19th-century poet and magazine editor

The essence of morality is a questioning about morality; and the decisive move of human life is to use ceaselessly all light to look for the origin of the opposition between good and evil.

— Georges Bataille, French essayist and philosopher

The beauty of the soul shines out when a man bears with composure one heavy mischance after another, not because he does not feel them, but because he is a man of high and heroic temper.

— Aristotle, ancient Greek philosopher

The infliction of cruelty with a good conscience is the delight of moralists—that is why they invented hell.

— Bertrand Russell, British philosopher

A good conscience is to the soul what health is to the body; it preserves constant ease and serenity within us; and more than countervails all the calamities and afflictions which can befall us from without.

— *Joseph Addison, 17th-century English essayist*

What we have in us of the image of God is the love of truth and justice.

— *Demosthenes, 4th-century B.C. Greek orator*

Nearly all men can stand adversity, but if you want to test a man's character, give him power.

— *Abraham Lincoln, American president and lawyer*

There is one thing alone that stands the brunt of life throughout its course: a quiet conscience.

— *Euripides, ancient Greek playwright and tragedian*

It is safe to say that no other superstition is so detrimental to growth, so enervating and paralyzing to the minds and hearts of the people, as the superstition of Morality.

— *Emma Goldman, Lithuanian-born anarchist and activist*

Morality comes with the sad wisdom of age, when the sense of curiosity has withered.

> — *Graham Greene, English novelist and playwright*

Every man, in his own opinion, forms an exception to the ordinary rules of morality.

> — *William Hazlitt, 18th-century English essayist*

What is moral is what you feel good after, and what is immoral is what you feel bad after.

> — *Ernest Hemingway, American novelist*

Morality is not the doctrine of how we may make ourselves happy, but how we may make ourselves worthy of happiness.

> — *Immanuel Kant, 18th-century German philosopher*

To give a man full knowledge of morality, I would send him to no other book than the New Testament.

> — *John Locke, 17th-century English philosopher*

It is not work that kills men; it is worry. Work is healthy; you can hardly put more upon a man than he can bear. Worry is rust upon the blade. It is not the revolution that destroys the machinery, but the friction. Fear secrets acids; but love and trust are sweet juices.

— *Henry Ward Beecher, 19th-century Protestant preacher and reformer*

It's silly to go on pretending that under the skin we are all brothers. The truth is more likely that under the skin we are all cannibals, assassins, traitors, liars, hypocrites, poltroons.

— *Henry Miller, American author and essayist*

Union of the weakest develops strength not wisdom. Can all men, together, avenge one of the leaves that have fallen in autumn? But the wise man avenges by building his city in snow.

— *Wallace Stevens, American poet*

Everywhere, the ethical predicament of our time imposes itself with an urgency which suggests that even the question "Have we anything to eat?" will be answered not in material but in ethical terms.

— *Hugo Ball, German-born Dada artist, poet, and stage director*

But who prays for Satan? Who, in eighteen centuries, has had the common humanity to pray for the one sinner that needed it most?

— Mark Twain, 19th-century American writer and humorist

Moralities, ethics, laws, customs, beliefs, doctrines—these are of trifling import. All that matters is that the miraculous become the norm.

— Henry Miller, American author and essayist

15. art and creativity

Art is lies that tell the truth.

— *Pablo Picasso, Spanish painter*

It is generally recognized that creativity requires leisure, an absence of rush, time for the mind and imagination to float and wander and roam, time for the individual to descend into the depths of his or her psyche, to be available to barely audible signals rustling for attention. Long periods of time may pass in which nothing seems to be happening. But we know that kind of space must be created if the mind is to leap out of its accustomed ruts, to part from the mechanical, the known, the familiar, the standard, and generate a leap into the new.

— *Nathaniel Branden, American author and psychotherapist*

Another unsettling element in modern art is that common symptom of immaturity, the dread of doing what has been done before.

— *Edith Wharton, 19th-century American novelist*

Works of art, in my opinion, are the only objects in the material universe to possess internal order, and that is why, though I don't believe that only art matters, I do believe in Art for Art's sake.

— E.M. Forster, English novelist

All art is a kind of confession, more or less oblique. All artists, if they are to survive, are forced at last, to tell whole story: to vomit the anguish up.

— James Baldwin, African-American novelist

It is art that makes life, makes interest, makes importance and I know of no substitute whatever for the force and beauty of its process.

— Henry James, American novelist

Art is the human disposition of sensible or intelligible matter for an aesthetic end.

— James Joyce, Irish novelist

Art is a human activity having for its purpose the transmission to others of the highest and best feelings to which men have risen.

— Leo Tolstoy, 19th-century Russian novelist

What seems to me the highest and the most difficult achievement of Art is not to make us laugh or cry, or to rouse our lust or our anger, but to do as nature does—that is, fill us with wonderment.

— *Gustave Flaubert, 19th-century French novelist*

I can't bear art that you can walk round and admire. A book should be either a bandit or a rebel or a man in the crowd.

— *D.H. Lawrence, English novelist and poet*

Our species is the only creative species, and it has only one creative instrument, the individual mind and spirit of a man. Nothing was ever created by two men. There are no good collaborations, whether in music, in art, in poetry, in mathematics, in philosophy. Once the miracle of creation has taken place, the group can build and extend it, but the group never invents anything. The preciousness lies in the lonely mind of a man.

— *John Steinbeck, American novelist*

Art should be appreciated with passion and violence, not with a tepid, deprecating elegance that fears the censoriousness of a common room.

— *W. Somerset Maugham, French-born novelist and playwright*

The true function of art is to... edit nature and so make it coherent and lovely. The artist is a sort of impassioned proofreader, blue-penciling the bad spelling of God.

— *H.L. Mencken, American journalist and essayist*

Art is the communication of ecstasy.

— *Peter Ouspensky, Russian-born philosopher*

Art is a collaboration between God and the artist, and the less the artist does, the better.

— *Andre Gide, French writer and critic*

A true artist will let his wife starve, his children go barefoot, his mother drudge for a living at 70, sooner than work at anything but his art.

— *George Bernard Shaw, Irish playwright and essayist*

Only through art can we emerge from ourselves and know what another person sees.

— *Marcel Proust, French novelist*

Creativity comes from trust. Trust your instincts. And never hope more than you work.

— *Rita Mae Brown, American writer and feminist activist*

In the case of many poets, the most important thing for them to do... is to write as little as possible.

— *T.S. Eliot, American-born poet*

A man is always a teller of tales, he lives surrounded by his stories and the stories of others, he sees everything that happens to him through them; and he tries to live his life as if he were recounting it.

— *Jean-Paul Sartre, French philosopher and playwright*

Stories ought not to be just little bits of fantasy that are used to wile away an idle hour; from the beginning of the human race stories have been used—by priests, by bards, by medicine men—as magic instruments of healing, of teaching, as a means of helping people come to terms with the fact that they continually have to face insoluble problems and unbearable realities.

— *Joan Aiken, English fantasy novelist*

There is no greater agony than bearing an untold story inside you.

— *Maya Angelou, American poet*

The story—from Rumplestiltskin to War and Peace—is one of the basic tools invented by the human mind, for the purpose of gaining understanding. There have been great societies that did not use the wheel, but there have been no societies that did not tell stories.

— *Ursula K. LeGuin, American science-fiction writer*

The essence of all art is to have pleasure in giving pleasure.

— *Mikhail Baryshnikov, Russian ballet dancer*

The more a man cultivates the arts the less he fornicates. A more and more apparent cleavage occurs between the spirit and the brute.

— *Charles Baudelaire, 19th-century French Symbolist poet*

In order for the artist to have a world to express he must first be situated in this world, oppressed or oppressing, resigned or rebellious, a man among men.

— *Simone de Beauvoir, French essayist and feminist*

I like to write when I feel spiteful; it's like having a good sneeze.

— D.H. Lawrence, English novelist and poet

The work of art, just like any fragment of human life considered in its deepest meaning, seems to me devoid of value if it does not offer the hardness, the rigidity, the regularity, the luster on every interior and exterior facet, of the crystal.

— Andre Breton, French poet and critic

Fine art, that exists for itself alone, is art in a final state of impotence. If nobody, including the artist, acknowledges art as a means of knowing the world, then art is relegated to a kind of rumpus room of the mind and the irresponsibility of the artist and the irrelevance of art to actual living becomes part and parcel of the practice of art.

— Angela Carter, English novelist

Art is good when it springs from necessity. This kind of origin is the guarantee of its value; there is no other.

— Neal Cassady, Beat Generation literary figure

Religion and art spring from the same root and are close kin.
Economics and art are strangers.

     — *Willa Cather, 19th-century American novelist*

When I judge art, I take my painting and put it next to a God-made object like a tree or flower. If it clashes, it is not art.

     — *Marc Chagall, Russian-born painter*

The dignity of the artist lies in his duty of keeping awake the sense of wonder in the world. In this long vigil he often has to vary his methods of stimulation; but in this long vigil he is also himself striving against a continual tendency to sleep.

     — *G.K. Chesterton, English essayist and author*

Art is merely the refuge which the ingenious have invented, when they were supplied with food and women, to escape the tediousness of life.

     — *W. Somerset Maugham, French-born novelist and playwright*

Fortunately art is a community effort—a small but select community living in a spiritualized world endeavoring to interpret the wars and the solitudes of the flesh.

     — *Allen Ginsberg, American Beat poet*

Art is so wonderfully irrational, exuberantly pointless, but necessary all the same. Pointless and yet necessary, that's hard for a puritan to understand.

— *Gunter Grass, Polish-born German novelist*

Irresponsibility is part of the pleasure of all art; it is the part the schools cannot recognize.

— *Pauline Kael, film critic*

The aim of every artist is to arrest motion, which is life, by artificial means and hold it fixed so that a hundred years later, when a stranger looks at it, it moves again since it is life. Since man is mortal, the only immortality possible for him is to leave something behind him that is immortal since it will always move. This is the artist's way of scribbling "Kilroy was here" on the wall of the final and irrevocable oblivion through which he must someday pass.

— *William Faulkner, American novelist*

I see little of more importance to the future of our country and of civilization than full recognition of the place of the artist. If art is to nourish the roots of our culture, society must set the artist free to follow his vision wherever it takes him.

— *John F. Kennedy, American president and politician*

Art is science made clear.

— Jean Cocteau, French poet, playwright, and filmmaker

Art is the child of Nature; yes, her darling child, in whom we trace the features of the mother's face, her aspect and her attitude.

— Henry Wadsworth Longfellow, 19th-century American poet

A work of art that contains theories is like an object on which the price tag has been left.

— Marcel Proust, French novelist

There is the falsely mystical view of art that assumes a kind of supernatural inspiration, a possession by universal forces unrelated to questions of power and privilege or the artist's relation to bread and blood. In this view, the channel of art can only become clogged and misdirected by the artist's concern with merely temporary and local disturbances. The song is higher than the struggle.

— Adrienne Rich, American poet

I wrote the book because we're all gonna die.

— Jack Kerouac, American Beat novelist and poet

Not even the visionary or mystical experience ever lasts very long. It is for art to capture that experience, to offer it to, in the case of literature, its readers; to be, for a secular, materialist culture, some sort of replacement for what the love of god offers in the world of faith.

— *Salman Rushdie, Indian-born novelist*

A primary function of art and thought is to liberate the individual from the tyranny of his culture in the environmental sense and to permit him to stand beyond it in an autonomy of perception and judgment.

— *Lionel Trilling, American literary critic and essayist*

Poetry and progress are like two ambitious men who hate one another with an instinctive hatred, and when they meet upon the same road, one of them has to give place.

— *Charles Baudelaire, 19th-century French Symbolist poet*

Poetry is not an expression of the party line. It's that time of night, lying in bed, thinking what you really think, making the private world public, that's what the poet does.

— *Allen Ginsberg, American Beat poet*

I passionately hate the idea of being with it, I think an artist has always to be out of step with his time.

— *Orson Welles, American actor and film director*

I really do inhabit a system in which words are capable of shaking the entire structure of government, where words can prove mightier than ten military divisions.

— *Vaclav Havel, Czech playwright and president*

Eeyore was saying to himself, "This writing business. Pencils and what-not. Over-rated, if you ask me. Silly stuff. Nothing in it."

— *A.A. Milne, English children's writer*

Art is the symbol of the two noblest human efforts: to construct and to refrain from destruction.

— *Simone Weil, French philosopher*

Through all the world there goes one long cry from the heart of the artist: Give me leave to do my utmost.

— *Isak Dinesen, Danish-born novelist*

Creativity is allowing yourself to make mistakes. Art is knowing which ones to keep.

— *Scott Adams, American cartoonist*

One ought, every day at least, to hear a little song, read a good poem, see a fine picture, and if it were possible, to speak a few reasonable words.

— *Johann Wolfgang von Goethe, German poet and novelist*

The poet judges not as a judge judges but as the sun falling around a helpless thing.

— *Walt Whitman, American poet*

For the majority of creative people, life is a mean trick.

— *F. Scott Fitzgerald, American novelist*

The difference between Art and Life is that Art is more bearable.

— *Charles Bukowski, American novelist*

Times are bad. Children no longer obey their parents, and everyone is writing a book.

— *Marcus Cicero, Roman orator and writer*

Another unsettling element in modern art is that common symptom of immaturity, the dread of doing what has been done before.

— *Edith Wharton, 19th-century American novelist*

Works of art, in my opinion, are the only objects in the material universe to possess internal order, and that is why, though I don't believe that only art matters, I do believe in Art for Art's sake.

— *E.M. Forster, English novelist*

The creation of something new is not accomplished by the intellect but by the play instinct acting from inner necessity. The creative mind plays with the objects it loves.

— *Carl Jung, Swiss psychiatrist*

Creativity represents a miraculous coming together of the uninhibited energy of the child with its apparent opposite and enemy, the sense of order imposed on the disciplined adult intelligence.

— *Norma Podhoretz, American writer, editor, and literary critic*

It is the creative potential itself in human beings that is the image of God.

— Mary Daly, American theologian and feminist writer

I myself do nothing. The Holy Spirit accomplishes all through me.

— William Blake, 18th-century artist, poet, and mystic

resources

Books

Bartlett, John and Kaplan, Justin.
Bartlett's Familiar Quotations, Sixteenth Edition. Little, Brown, 1992.

Bly, Robert; Hillman, James; and Meade, Michael.
The Rag and Bone Shop of the Heart. HarperCollins, 1992.

Carroll, Andrew. *Letters of a Nation.* Broadway Books, 1999.

The Columbia World of Quotations. Columbia University Press, 1996.

Fitzhenry, Robert I.
The Harper Book of Quotations, Third Edition. HarperCollins, 1993.

Kemp, Peter. *The Oxford Dictionary of Literary Quotations.*
Oxford University Press, 1997.

Knowles, Elizabeth. *The Oxford Dictionary of 20th-Century Quotations.*
Oxford University Press, 1998.

Miller, Henry. *Black Spring.* Grove Press, 1963.

The Portable Dorothy Parker. Penguin Books, 1976.

Web Sites

About – Women's History, Women's Voices
(http://womenshistory.about.com/library/qu/blqulist.htm)

Bartleby.com

BrainyQuote.com

Curious Quotes (www.curiousquotes.com)

Curmudgeon-Online (www.curmudgeon-online.com)

Famous Quotes and Famous Sayings Network (home.att.net/~quotations/)

Food Reference Website (www.foodreference.com)

Great-Quotes.com

Motivational Quotes (www.motivationalquotes.com/)

One Proverb (www.oneproverb.com/)

Project Gutenberg

Quotes of the Day (www.qotd.org)

Surf-in-the-Spirit (www.surfinthespirit.com/advice/)

The Quotations Page (www.quotationspage.com/)

ThinkExist.com

about the author

Michelle Heller was born in Burlington, Vermont, grew up in Binghamton, New York, and has lived in London, France, and New York City. She now resides in San Francisco, where she makes a study of meditations found on the walls of public bathrooms. She holds a degree in creative writing from Tufts University and has worked as a gallery assistant, museum researcher, book editor, proofreader, hotel maid, cocktail waitress, carousel operator, and Web copywriter.